Student Name: _____

The Virginia Experience
USA I
History to 1877

Written by Carole Marsh

Editorial Assistants: Terry Briggs, Diana Sullivan • Graphic Designer: Cecil Anderson

NEW EDITION!
Current Standards
Test scores have increased as much as 400%

©2004 Carole Marsh/Gallopade International. All Rights Reserved.

No part of this publication may be reproduced in whole or in part, stored in a retrieval system, or transmitted in any form or by any means, electronic, mechanical, photocopying, recording or otherwise, without written permission from the publisher.

~ This book is not reproducible. ~

The Virginia Experience

Published by

GALLOPADE INTERNATIONAL

800-536-2GET
www.gallopade.com

ISBN
• 0-635-01066-6 •

©2004 Carole Marsh • All Rights Reserved.
No part of this publication may be reproduced in whole or in part,
stored in a retrieval system, or transmitted in any form or by any means,
electronic, mechanical, photocopying, recording or otherwise,
without written permission from the publisher.

*Gallopade is proud to be a member of the National Council for the Social Studies,
as well as these educational organizations and associations:*

Carole Marsh Virginia Titles

Virginia Experience Grade-Specific Readers—Famous People in the SOL

Addams, Jane
Anthony, Susan B.
Appleseed, Johnny
Ashe, Arthur
Byrd, Harry Flood
Brown, John
Cabot, John
Cartier, Jacques
Carver, George Washington
Champlain, Samuel de
Crockett, Davy
Columbus, Christopher
Franklin, Benjamin
Grant, Ulysses S.
Henry, Patrick
Jackson, Thomas "Stonewall"
James I, King
Jefferson, Thomas
Jones, John Paul
Keller, Helen
King, Martin Luther, Jr.
Lafayette, Marquis de
Lee, Robert E.
Lincoln, Abraham
Madison, James
Marshall, Thurgood
Mason, George
Monroe, James
Newport, Christopher
Parks, Rosa
Ponce de Leon, Juan
Pocahontas
Powell Jr., Lewis F.
Powhatan, Chief
Revere, Paul
Rolfe, John
Robinson, Jackie
Ross, Betsy
Smith, Captain John
Stuart, J.E.B.
Tubman, Harriet
Turner, Nat
Walker, Maggie Lena
Washington, Booker T.
Washington, George
Wilder, L. Douglas
Wilson, Woodrow
Wythe, George

The Virginia Experience Kindergarten Student Workbook
The Virginia Experience Kindergarten Teacher Resource
The Virginia Experience First Grade Student Workbook
The Virginia Experience First Grade Teacher Resource
The Virginia Experience Second Grade Student Workbook
The Virginia Experience Second Grade Teacher Resource
The Virginia Experience Third Grade Student Workbook
The Virginia Experience Third Grade Teacher Resource
The Virginia Experience Virginia Studies Workbook
The Virginia Experience Virginia Studies Teacher Resource
The Virginia Experience United States History I Workbook
The Virginia Experience United States History I Teacher Resource
The Virginia Experience United States History II Workbook
The Virginia Experience United States History II Teacher Resource
The Virginia Experience Standards of Learning Reference Guide
The Virginia Experience Poster/Map
The Virginia Experience Civics for Teachers
The Virginia Experience Economics for Teachers
20 Ways to Teach the SOL with PIZZAZZ!
A Virginia Mystery Musical!
The Virginia Experience Tee Shirt
The Virginia Experience Pencils
The Virginia Experience Biographies Book—All the Famous People in the SOL
Pass The Test! CD-ROM Kindergarten—Social Studies
Pass The Test! CD-ROM First Grade—Social Studies
Pass The Test! CD-ROM Second Grade—Social Studies
Pass The Test! CD-ROM Third Grade—Social Studies
Pass The Test! CD-ROM Virginia Studies
Virginia Facts & Factivities! CD-ROM (Lesson Plans, Reproducible Activities, & Teacher's Guide also available)
Let's Discover Virginia! CD-ROM
The BIG Virginia Reproducible Activity Book
My First Book About Virginia!
Virginia Jeopardy!: Answers & Questions About Our State
Virginia "Jography!": A Fun Run Through Our State
My First Pocket Guide: Virginia
The Very Virginia Coloring Book
Virginia Stickers
Virginia Biography Bingo Game
Virginia Geography Bingo Game
Virginia History Bingo Game

A Word from the Author...

Dear Student,

Welcome to the USA! In this book, you will find information about this country from before the first explorers reached its shores until after the Civil War ended up to 1877. You may be studying this period in U.S. history for the very first time, or you may be reviewing for your Standards of Learning test. In either case, this workbook will make your studying faster and more fun!

As you progress in school, you will find that your USA Studies will prepare you to understand people and places around the world. Why? Because you will already possess a wealth of knowledge about how things work–history, geography, politics, and more!

How exciting it is to study the greatest country in the world! Have you ever thought about how geography affected the way this nation was settled? Have you ever wondered how the early inhabitants overcame major obstacles to create a nation? Have you ever considered what a task it was for the founding fathers to create a new government with only their knowledge of how European countries were governed or considered the many opinions that were being voiced at the time?

As the nation grew, other challenges arose for Americans. Some were so great that states separated from the Union, formed their own country, and declared war on the Union. Once the war was over, the nation had to be reassembled. It was a difficult time, but the entire United States has once again risen to a level of greatness that is envied by many other nations.

I've learned a lot by researching and writing USA books and other products about our great nation. It is my hope that you will learn a lot, too! Come along with me and enjoy your very own journey through our nation's interesting past. And, remember, learning is fun!

Carole Marsh

Table of Contents

Icon Identification	6
Section I ~ Geography: From Lowlands to Mountains...	7
Section II ~ Geography: How Early Cultures Developed...	20
Section III ~ History: New Lands to Explore and Conquer	27
Section IV ~ History and Geography: Factors That Shaped...	45
Section V ~ History and Civics: Causes and Results of...	59
Section VI ~ History and Civics: Challenges of a New Nation	83
Section VII ~ History, Geography, and Economics: Expanding...	97
Section VIII ~ History, Geography, and Economics: Civil War...	113
Section IX ~ History and Civics: Effects of Reconstruction...	141
Section X ~ Extra Credit	147
Fifty Nifty States	148
Practice Test	149
Section XI ~ Appendix	151
Virginia Timeline	152
USA Glossary	154
Maps	155
Index	158
About the Author / Notes About Answer Key	160

Icon Identification

Hard-To-Believe-But-True!
Fascinating trivia!

Map Skill Builder
Learn map skills and never be lost!

Question for Discussion
Who wants to be a millionaire?!

Reading Activity
The best kind of activity!

Scavenger Hunt!
Stuff for you to look for!

Math Experience
A neat math problem or info!

Quick Quiz
Think fast!

Special Economics Info
Money Makes the World Go 'Round!

Origin/Definition
Word origins or definitions.

The Great Debate
A chance to share your opinion!

Background Check
Deep digging unearthed this stuff!

Look-It-Up!
We can't give you EVERYTHING!

Enrichment
Stuff that will stick with you!

High Tech
Computer Technology Connections!

Special Civics Information

Quick Review
You didn't forget, did you?

Write About It!
A writing activity.

Scratch Pad
A place for calculations... or doodles!

One More - Just for Fun!
All work and no play...

Essential Skills
You can't live without these!

~ This book is not reproducible. ~

Section 1

Geography:
From Lowlands to Mountains, Rivers to Oceans

Chapter 1

*Standard USI.2a—Locate the seven continents.
Correlates with US1.1f.*

Continental and Monumental

Continents are large land masses surrounded by water. There are seven continents on Earth. The seven continents are North America, South America, Africa, Asia, Australia, Antarctica, and Europe.

Europe is not entirely surrounded by water, but it is still considered a continent. Europe is located next to Asia. The large land mass that includes Europe and Asia is sometimes called Eurasia.

You can see what the continents look like by looking at maps and globes. Satellites take photographs of the Earth from outer space. They provide photographs of what the continents look like. Tables can be used to identify the continents. For example, a table may list the continents in order of largest to smallest, or from the most populated to the least populated.

Below is a table listing the continents and their sizes.

CONTINENT	SIZE IN SQUARE MILES
Africa	11,677,240
Antarctica	5,500,000
Asia	17,139,000
Australia	2,967,877
Europe	4,000,000
North America	9,400,000
South America	6,880,000

On the map on page 9, put the continents in order by size from the largest to smallest. Use this space for notes.

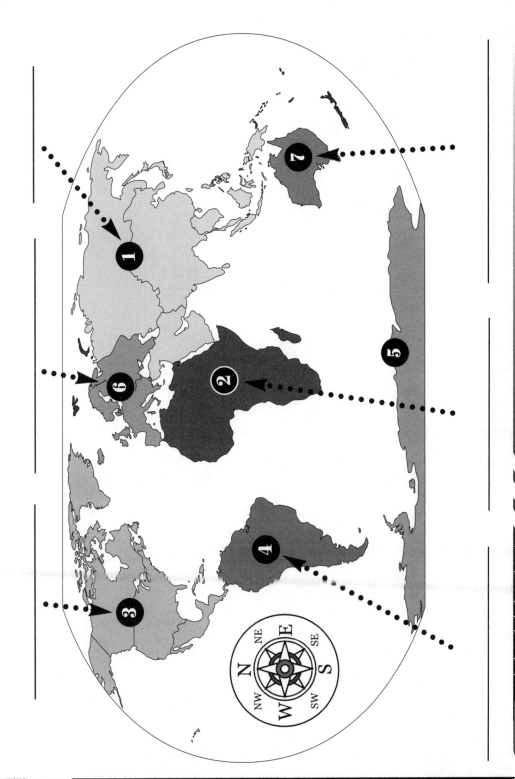

Each continent is numbered in size from largest to smallest. Using the information from the table and your notes, you should be able to determine which continent is which on the map above based on its size. Label the continents.

Look at a globe and see if you can identify each of the seven continents. As you find them on the globe, label them on this map.

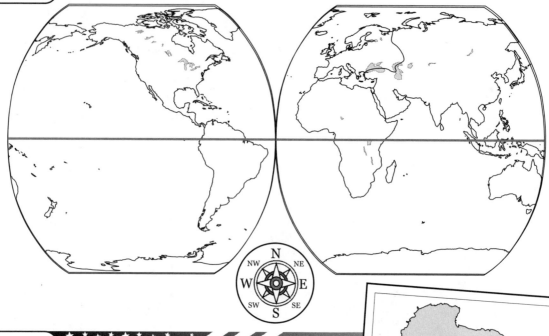

 This picture shows the continent that is sometimes called the "bottom of the world." Write this continent's name on the map.

The Bottom of the World

 This picture shows two continents even though they are often referred to as just one. The two separate continents are

_____ and

_____ .

Together, they're referred to as

_____ .

Two for One

Chapter 2

Standard USI.2b—Locate and describe the location of North America's geographic regions. Correlates with USI.1f.

Geographic Formations

Geographic regions have distinctive characteristics. The continent of North America has eight geographic regions determined by landforms and bodies of water.

Coastal Plain—along the Atlantic Ocean and the Gulf of Mexico; broad lowland with many excellent harbors.

Appalachian Highlands—west of the Coastal Plain, from eastern Canada to western Alabama including the Piedmont; eroded mountains; North America's oldest range.

Canadian Shield—horseshoe shape wrapping around Hudson Bay; hills worn by erosion and hundreds of glacier-carved lakes; some of the oldest rock formations in North America.

Interior Lowlands—west of the Appalachian Mountains and east of the Great Plains; lowlands with rolling flatlands, rivers, broad river valleys, and grassy hills.

Great Plains—west of Interior Lowlands and east of the Rocky Mountains; flat lands that slightly increase in elevation westward; known for grasslands.

Rocky Mountains—west of the Great Plains and east of the Basin and Range; rugged mountains with high elevations stretching from Alaska almost to Mexico; includes Continental Divide, which determines the directional flow of rivers.

Basin and Range—west of the Rocky Mountains and east of the Sierra Nevadas and the Cascades; includes varying elevations and isolated mountain ranges, and Death Valley—the lowest point in North America.

Coastal Range—Pacific Coast stretching from California to Canada; rugged mountains and fertile valleys.

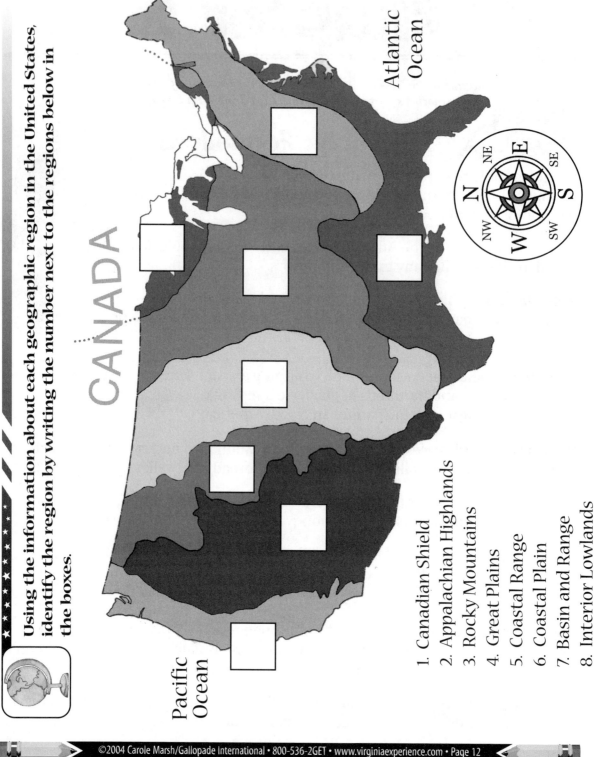

Look at each picture or photograph and decide what region it is from. Write your answers on the line under each picture.

long, sandy beaches	Death Valley	rolling hills, rivers	glacier-covered lakes

old, eroded mountains	most western region	grasslands	Continental Divide

Chapter 3

Standard USI.2c—Locate and identify water features important to the early history of the United States. Correlates with USI.1a, USI.1c, USI.1f, and USI.2c

 ## The Water Brought Them There!

The United States has access to many different bodies of water. Bodies of water have been important in the nation's history because they have supported interaction among the regions, formed borders, and created links to other areas. They have been useful for trade, transportation, and settlement.

Major bodies of water in the United States include two oceans: the Atlantic and the Pacific. The nation's many rivers include the Mississippi, the Missouri, the Rio Grande, the Columbia, the Ohio, and the Colorado. The Great Lakes are in the North, and the Gulf of Mexico is in the South.

From Oceans to Rivers, They Explored

The Atlantic and Pacific oceans provided the United States with access to other areas of the world. The Atlantic Ocean served as a highway for explorers, early settlers, and immigrants who arrived later. The Pacific Ocean was also an early exploration route.

The first European explorers to reach North America were from England and Spain. They sailed across the Atlantic Ocean, reaching the eastern coast of North America beginning in the mid-1400s.

The first sighting of the Pacific Ocean by a European may have taken place in 1513, when the Spanish conquistador Vasco Nuñez de Balboa and his party made their way from Panama. They reported finding the "Southern Sea," or what is today called the Pacific Ocean.

The Gulf of Mexico provided the Spanish and French with exploration routes to Mexico and other parts of America. In 1528, the Spanish explorer Alvar Nuñez Cabeza de Vaca sailed up the Gulf of Mexico and had a part in the settlement of Galveston, Texas. His exploration showed the Spanish that the land north of Mexico was much larger than they had believed.

Put the following bodies of water in order of the time in which they were first sailed by explorers. Write the numbers 1, 2, and 3 in the proper blanks.

___ Atlantic Ocean   ___ Gulf of Mexico   ___ Pacific Ocean

In 1528, de Vaca and three others from his party were captured by Indians. They were basically kept as slaves for more than six years. Finally, they escaped! With no clothes or supplies, they traveled hundreds of miles on foot until they finally reached a camp of Spanish soldiers in Mexico. They became well known for their bravery.

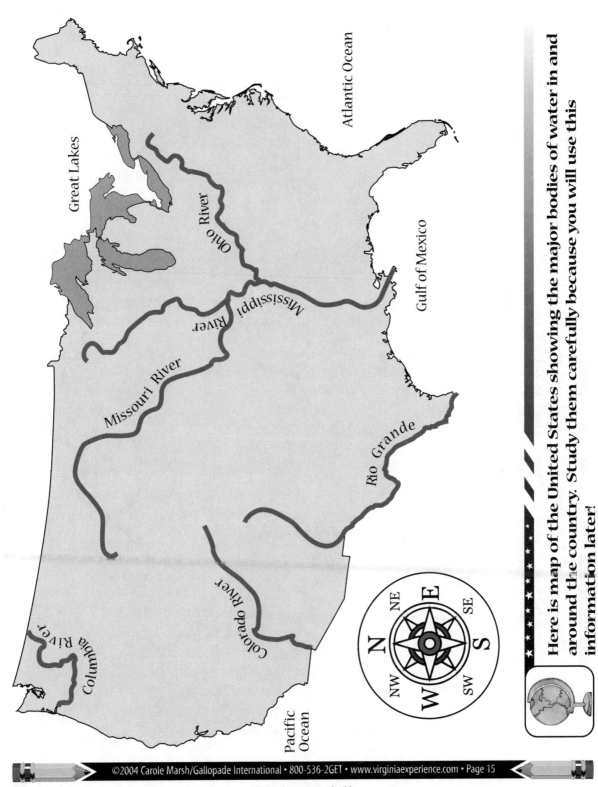

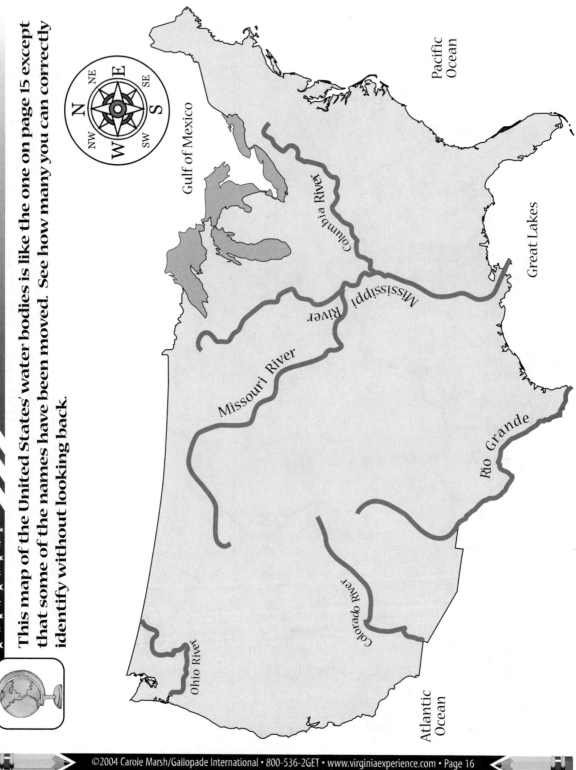

A River Runs Through It

Rivers have been important to the United States from historical and geographical perspectives. Lewis and Clark followed the Columbia River in the early 1800s when they were mapping out the Louisiana Purchase. The Columbia River became an important route on the way west toward the Pacific Ocean.

The Spanish were the first Europeans to explore the Colorado River. In 1540, Hernando de Alarcón sailed his Spanish galleon upriver to the point we know today as Yuma, Arizona.

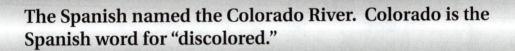

The Spanish named the Colorado River. Colorado is the Spanish word for "discolored."

The Rio Grande forms the United States' border between Texas and Mexico. The Spanish also explored this river.

The Mississippi and Missouri rivers were transportation arteries for farms and industries, and they linked the United States to ports and other parts of the world. The Ohio River was the gateway to the west. In the early 1800s, it became the main artery for settlers pouring into the West.

Many inland port cities also grew in the Midwest along the banks of the Great Lakes, including cities such as Detroit, Michigan and Chicago, Illinois. These cities became major industrial and commercial centers that are still important to our nation's economy today.

When Lewis and Clark were exploring the Columbia River, they were amazed by the number of salmon in the river. On a good day of fishing, a man could catch a hundred fish! They also noted how clear the water of the river was. No matter how deep it was, they could see the river bottom!

Write TRADE or SETTLEMENT to describe how each body of water was used.

Goods ship to and from U.S. _____

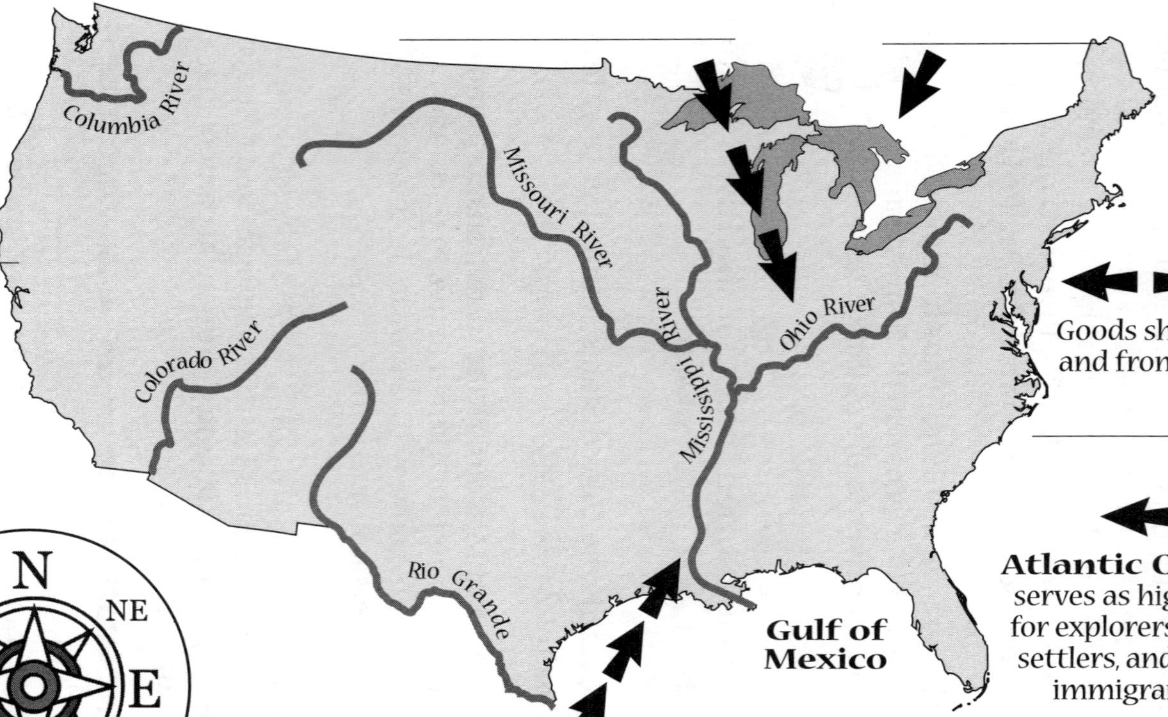

Inland port cities grew along Great Lakes _____

Atlantic Ocean serves as highway for explorers, early settlers, and later immigrants _____

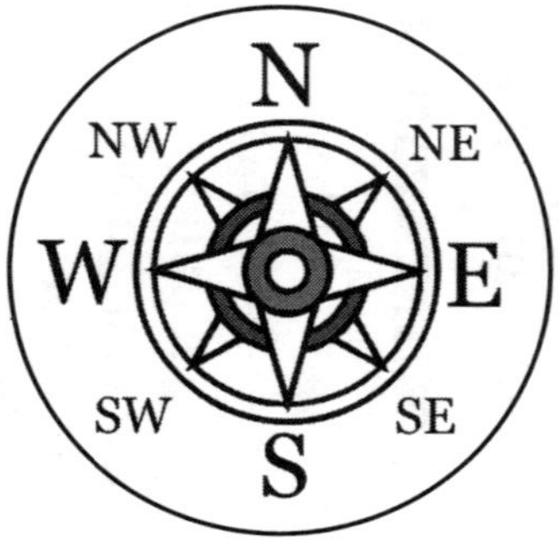

Gateway for moving people and goods to the west _____

Missouri and Mississippi rivers move farm and industrial products and link ports around the world _____

Goods ship to and from U.S. _____

Map labels: Ohio River, Mississippi River, Missouri River, Rio Grande, Colorado River, Columbia River, Gulf of Mexico, Pacific Ocean

Getting the Sources Straight

primary source document: an original document written by someone at the time an event is happening

Primary source documents can be letters, diaries, or journals. Primary source documents sometimes use words like "I," "we," and "our." Primary source documents can be also be papers like the Declaration of Independence or treaties.

secondary source document: written after an event takes place but uses a primary source document for information

Secondary source documents can be written long after the event occurs. Encyclopedias and some text in history books are examples of secondary source documents.

Which of these are examples of primary source documents, and which are secondary? **Write P on the line beside primary and S on the line beside secondary.**

1. ____ Then we set out to sea again, coasting towards the River of Palms. Every day our thirst and hunger increased because our supplies were giving out, as well as the water supply.

2. ____ Lewis and Clark traced the route of the Columbia River to the Pacific Ocean.

3. ____ From 1605 until 1608, Samuel de Champlain explored the coast of North America from Maine to Martha's Vineyard. He discovered most of the major rivers and drew the best maps of the coast.

4. ____ Great joy in camp! We are in view of the ocean, this great Pacific Ocean which we have been so long anxious to see!

Section II

Geography:
How Early Cultures Developed in the U.S.

Chapter 4

Standard USI.3a—Learn how early cultures in North America developed by locating where they settled. Correlates with USI.1c and USI.1f.

They Were Here First!

Before the European explorers arrived, American Indians, also known as First Americans, spread out and settled many areas across different environments in North America.

The Inuit inhabited present-day Alaska and northern Canada. They lived in Arctic areas where the temperature is below freezing much of the year. The Kwakiutl inhabited the Pacific Northwest coast. This area is usually rainy with a mild climate. The Sioux settled in the interior of the United States, called the Great Plains. This area is dry and has grasslands. The Pueblo inhabited the Southwest in present-day New Mexico and Arizona. They lived in deserts and areas bordering cliffs and mountains. The Iroquois inhabited northeast North America in the heavily forested region known as the Eastern Woodlands.

Check the group who lived in North America first.

____ Spanish explorers   ____ Iroquois Americans Indians

Experts believe that the first people to come to North America may have come across a frozen bridge of land that once connected Asia and Alaska. These people were called the Paleo-Indians. These early people were hunters who moved around according to the availability of food. They hunted and fished when they could and they gathered fruits and nuts.

Which group of American Indians settled in each area numbered on the map? Write your answer on the lines.

1 _____   3 _____
2 _____   4 _____
                         5 _____

Bering Land Bridge

WORD BANK
Inuit
Kwakiutl
Sioux
Pueblo
Iroquois

Circle the area that is the coldest most of the time.

Make a √ on the area that is a dry desert.

Put an X on the heavily forested area.

Draw a box around the region that has a mild, rainy climate.

Put a G on the dry grassland area.

Which do you think was the first group of American Indians to settle in North America? Why do you think they settled where they did?

Chapter 5

Standard USI.3b—Describe how the American Indians used their environment to obtain food, clothing, and shelter. Correlates with USI.1a, USI.1d, and USI.1f.

Where We Live Determines How We Live

Geography and climate affected how the groups of First Americans met their basic needs. Basic needs are things people must have to survive, such as clothes, food, and shelter. The First Americans hunted, fished, and farmed for food. Their clothing was made from animal skins and plants. They made homes from resources in their environment, including sod, stones, animal skins, and wood.

Fish, meat, corn, and roots

In the Northwest and coastal regions, tribes fished for food. In the Great Plains, the First Americans mainly hunted. The Pueblo grew some food, but also survived on wild plants. The Iroquois farmed, while tribes living in the Arctic region fished and hunted.

Sticks, stones, hides, and mud

The First Americans made shelters from materials around them. In the Arctic, they used blocks of ice. The Iroquois built longhouses, using a log frame covered with bark; these homes were shared by many people. The Pueblo built complex stone or clay structures on cliff sides. The Northwest tribes used timber to make plank houses. The Plains people had shelters they could pack up and move easily. They used wooden poles as a frame and covered them in buffalo hides.

 Look at these artifacts from the American Indians. Next to each, write which tribe you think may have used it.

_____   _____   _____

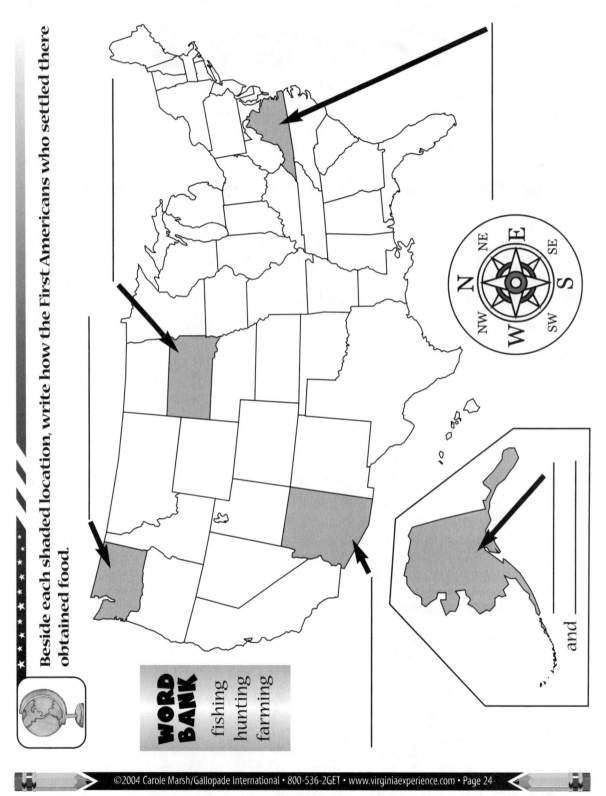

Various types of American Indians dwellings are shown here. **Beside each, write down who made these dwellings.**

 Igloo

_____

 Longhouse

_____

 Pueblo

_____

 Teepee

_____

Fashion statements

American Indians used what they could find to make clothing. In areas where the climate allowed plants to grow, they used plant fiber. This was most common in the southeastern areas. In extremely warm areas, they often wore little or no clothing, if any at all. When the weather turned cooler, they wore hides and furs for warmth. The Pueblo learned to grow cotton and used this to make clothing. The Indians of the Plains and those of the Arctic mainly wore hides and furs. Tribes of the Pacific Northwest wore various clothing made of plant materials, hides, and fur, since all were readily available in their area.

 Below is a chart of Native American tribes. From the information and your own analysis, fill in the chart. A few are done for you.

TRIBES	LOCATION	Obtaining FOOD	Clothing MATERIALS	Housing MATERIALS
Inuit				
Kwakiutl		Fished		
Sioux			Fur, hides	
Pueblo				Adobe, stone
Iroquois	Eastern Woodlands			

Now that you've exercised your mind and learned about the land and some of the early peoples of North America, it's time for a little fun!
Find the hidden words.

```
E L C D C A C Q A T G M C C R
E J T B F E L T J L S O I H E
E X L U B E L A E X C W F A V
R Q P E I A J W S I F X I M I
P M U L N K I L X K H V C P R
U Q M T O S A E N M A T A L O
E J I Y V R M W O T U I P A D
B C Q L J F E H K K R U L I A
L Y X X O W K R A L C N S N R
O R X F P X K O S H X I K S O
S L L U R C A N A D A O M M L
X U J X O W S I O U Q O R I O
G Y U B F I V H U N T Y B K C
D U P K J R S O Y P F A R M G
G R E A T L A K E S O F I S H
```

WORD BANK

ALASKA	CANADA	GREAT LAKES	KWAKIUTL
QUEBEC	CHAMPLAIN	GULF OF MEXICO	LEWIS
SIOUX	CLARK	INUIT	PACIFIC
PUEBLO	COLORADO RIVER	IROQUOIS	HUNT
ATLANTIC	EXPLORERS	FISH	FARM

©2004 Carole Marsh/Gallopade International • 800-536-2GET • www.virginiaexperience.com • Page 26

~ This book is not reproducible. ~

Section III

History:
New Lands to Explore and Conquer

Chapter 6

Standard US1.4a—Describe the motivations, obstacles, and accomplishments of Spanish, French, Portuguese, and English exploration. Correlates with USI.1a, USI.1d, and USI.1f.

Finders, Keepers!

As European explorers began to make voyages to the New World, major European countries such as Spain, France, Portugal, and England, were in competition to extend their power into North America and claim the land.

Many of the explorations were for economic reasons: the explorers were seeking riches, such as gold. For example, the Spanish conquistador Francisco Coronado was in search of gold when he explored the southwestern United States claiming the area for Spain.

In some cases, explorers hoped to find natural resources that would be valuable. John Cabot may have been the first European to land on the eastern coast of Canada. He returned to England with reports of bountiful supplies of fish and large forests of tall trees. The timber from the trees would be useful for ship masts. More than 100 years later, the French explorer Samuel de Champlain found great numbers of beaver when he reached the eastern coast of Canada. The fur trade was a profitable one at that time. Champlain established the French settlement of Quebec, which became a trading center in the New World.

Another reason for exploration was a desire to spread religion—especially Christianity—to other lands. Many explorers felt they had to conquer new lands to add to the size of the empire they represented. Many had a belief that their own culture was the best, and they felt the need to prove it.

Is the second paragraph of this chapter, which begins "Many of the explorations…" a primary or secondary source document?
_____

Fill in the blanks.

I am the Frenchman Samuel de Champlain. Do you know what animal I hoped to find in the New World?

_____

Do you know what settlement I founded?

_____

I am Francisco Coronado. Do you know what I was hoping to find?

_____

I am John Cabot. I sailed from England. When I reached the New World, I was impressed with the tall trees I found. What would these be good for making?

_____

Which Way Do We Go?

Exploring new regions wasn't an easy task. Imagine heading toward a place you've never been without a good map, or even a map at all! The explorers had very primitive navigational equipment, if they had any at all. Climates were sometimes different in the areas where they landed and food was not immediately available. Many men died of starvation. They also encountered diseases for which they had no immunities. Wild new areas presented challenges such as insects (which often carried diseases). Explorers often set out with inadequate supplies to last the journey or to carry them through until they became more familiar with the area where they had landed.

One of the greatest obstacles, however, may have been the basic fear of the unknown. What would they find once they reached land? Great stores of wealth and riches? Uninhabitable deserts? Hostile natives? These were risky ventures.

This map is like the one drawn by Samuel de Champlain. Is his map a primary or secondary source document? _____

The desire of some men to explore new worlds had its benefits. Exploration allowed goods and ideas to be exchanged by different peoples. As new explorations took place, navigational tools improved. New areas were mapped. Transportation also improved as the explorers made changes to their ships. The main accomplishment of exploration may have been how countries increased their land holdings throughout the New World.

Explore The New World!

Explorers from Spain, France, and England set out for North America. The Spanish explorer Francisco Coronado claimed the southwestern United States for Spain. French explorer Samuel de Champlain established the French settlement of Quebec, and another French explorer, Robert La Salle, claimed the Mississippi River Valley for his homeland. John Cabot, who sailed for England, explored eastern Canada. The Portuguese made voyages of discovery along West Africa.

Match each explorer with the country he represented.

1. ___ John Cabot
2. ___ Samuel de Champlain
3. ___ Francisco Coronado
4. ___ Robert La Salle

A. England
B. France
C. Spain

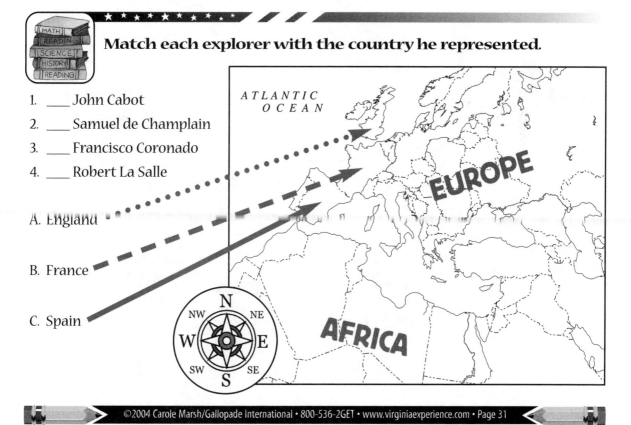

Look at each numbered area and write the name of the explorer(s) who claimed the area for his country. Use the Helpful HINTS box to help with the locations they explored.

① _____   ③ _____

② _____   ④ _____

Helpful HINTS:

Québec
•
Mississippi River Valley
•
eastern Canada
•
southwestern United States

Look at this map and draw a route a Portuguese explorer may have taken to West Africa. Use the compass rose to help you. What ocean did Portuguese explorers sail?

_____.

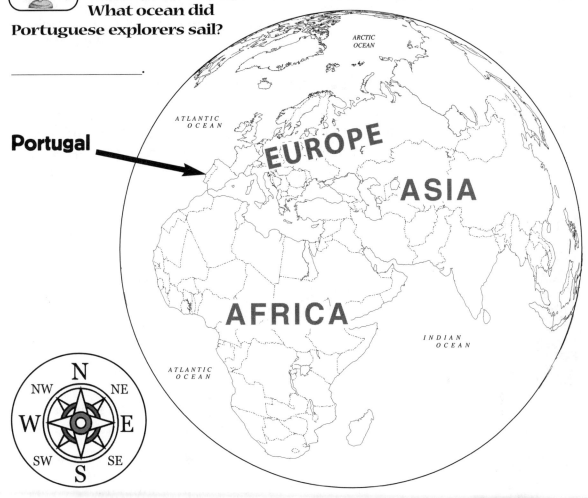

The ruler responsible for Portugal's exploration was Prince Henry, who was nicknamed "the Navigator." He sent many expeditions along the coast of West Africa, but they moved slowly…because the sailors were nervous. They believed the waters at the equator were at the boiling point, that human skin turned black, and that sea monsters would engulf ships!

~ This book is not reproducible. ~

Chapter 7

USI.4b—Describe cultural interactions between Europeans and American Indians that led to conflict and cooperation. Correlates with USI.1.a, and USI.1d.

Takers, Breakers!

When the European explorers reached North America, they found people already living there. These were tribes of American Indians, also called the First Americans. The interactions between the American Indians and the Europeans sometimes led to cooperation, but at other times, they resulted in conflict.

Here are ways the Europeans and American Indians interacted:

The FRENCH:
- established trading posts
- spread the Christian religion

The ENGLISH:
- established settlements
- claimed ownership of land
- learned farming techniques from the American Indians
- traded goods with the American Indians

The SPANISH:
- conquered and enslaved many American Indians
- brought Christianity to the New World
- brought European diseases

The areas of cooperation between the Europeans and First Americans can be summed up in three words: technologies, trade, and crops. Technologies involved transporting weapons and farm tools. The areas of conflict included claims to land, competition for trade, differences in culture, diseases from the Europeans, and differences in languages.

Look at these things the Europeans did in North America. Beside each, write which nation was responsible:

① _____ Established settlements

② _____ Conquered American Indians

③ _____ Established trading posts

④ _____ Learned farming techniques from American Indians

The European explorers were usually out for the three G's:
Gold, God, and Glory.

Think about the similarities and the differences between the Europeans and the First Americans using the information you have read.

Use this chart to illustrate the relationship between the European explorers and the First Americans. One is done to get you started.

AREAS OF COOPERATION	AREAS OF CONFLICT
crops	

Did the European explorers treat the First Americans fairly?
❏ Yes ❏ No   What made you reach your decision?

Here is a puzzle that shows a scene from the time when the explorers were sailing to North America. One piece has not been added. The two pieces show two different points of view.

Put an X on the piece that reflects the explorers' point of view.
Put a √ on the piece that shows the American Indians' point of view.

We are happy here. New people will come and they may change the way we live. That is frightening.

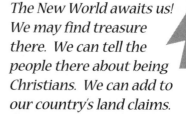

The New World awaits us! We may find treasure there. We can tell the people there about being Christians. We can add to our country's land claims.

Look at each of the journal entries. Based on what you know about the nations that explored the Americas, write which group would have made the journal entry.

1. The people living here are amazed by us. They ask about our weapons and our clothes. We have set up trading posts where they bring hides from game they have killed. In return for the hides, which we send home to be made into coats and hats, we give them small trinkets such as beads. Our trading posts are quite profitable.

   _____

2. The land here is plentiful and has not been developed. We shall claim it as ours in honor of our homeland. You know what they say: the early bird gets the worm!

   _____

3. They are just a bunch of savages living here in this wilderness. We can easily overpower them and make them into our slaves. They might even have hidden stores of gold we can take from them. There are so many of these Indians living here that we have a constant supply of slaves to do the hard work for us.

   _____

4. The land here is beautiful. We have plenty of water nearby and there are also many forests of large trees we can use to build houses and churches. This is a wonderful place for us to build settlements.

   _____

WORD BANK

Spanish

English

French

5. There were lots of Indians we could turn into slaves when we first arrived here, but the numbers have been going down. Many of them have been getting sick and dying from diseases like the ones we often saw at home.

   _____

Chapter 8

US1.4c—Describing the characteristics of the West African societies and their interactions with traders. Correlates with USI.1d, USI.1f, and USI.1g.

On to Africa!

While explorers were making their way to North America, things were taking place in the rest of the world as well. Several empires were dominant in West Africa during the exploration period of the 1400s and 1500s.

Between the years of 300 and 1600, Ghana, Mali, and Songhai each dominated West Africa at some point. These empires became powerful by controlling trade in that area of the world. The African people and African goods played an important role in making the Europeans interested in world resources.

The Portuguese were the main group to trade with the West Africans. They sailed south in the Atlantic Ocean until they reached their destination. They carried goods from Europe to the West African empires. They traded metals, cloth, and other manufactured goods for gold.

latitude: an imaginary line that joins points on the Earth's surface that are all equal distance north or south of the equator

longitude: the angular distance east or west of the prime meridian that stretches from the north pole to the south pole and passes through Greenwich, England

Very little is known about the early history of West Africa because there were not many written records. Even archaeologists looking into the area's past have had a hard time because the West Africans built their cities from materials that don't last a long time, such as grass, wood, and mud. The main way West Africa's history has been preserved is through oral tradition, by people passing on stories and songs time and time again.

On the globe below, use a blue marker to trace the lines of latitude. Use a red marker to trace the lines of longitude.

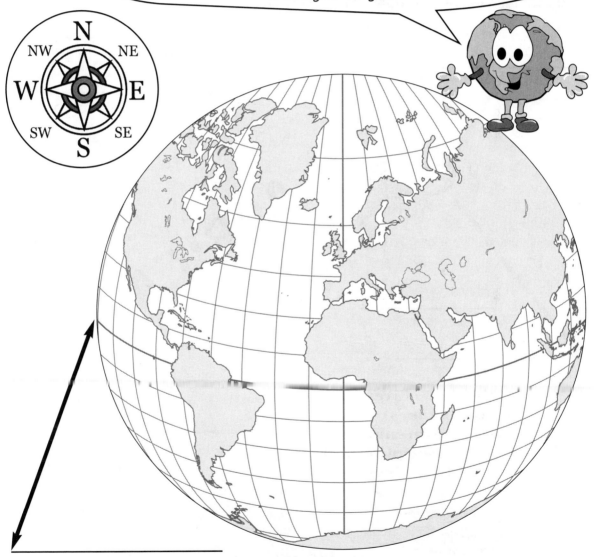

The equator is an imaginary line that runs east-west at the widest point on the Earth's surface. The empires of Mali, Ghana, and Songhai were just north of the equator. Label the equator on the drawing of the globe.

AFRICA! Where the Empires Were

Ghana was the smallest of the three West African empires. It was a small, round-shaped empire within the continent. It did not extend on its western side to the coast of the Atlantic Ocean. Mali extended from the Atlantic coast nearly a quarter of the way into the African continent. Mali was somewhat shaped like a rectangle. Songhai, the largest of the three empires, covered most of the area included in Ghana and Mali and extended nearly one-third of the width of Africa.

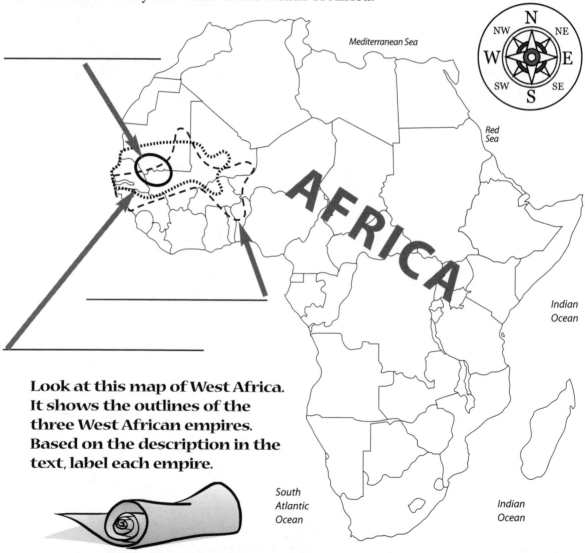

Look at this map of West Africa. It shows the outlines of the three West African empires. Based on the description in the text, label each empire.

Empire of Ghana

The first of the West African empires was Ghana, which hit its peak in the 1200s. Ghana was known for its rich supplies of gold and for the mineral salt, which was transported across the Sahara Desert. The salt was so valuable that it was used as currency, or money.

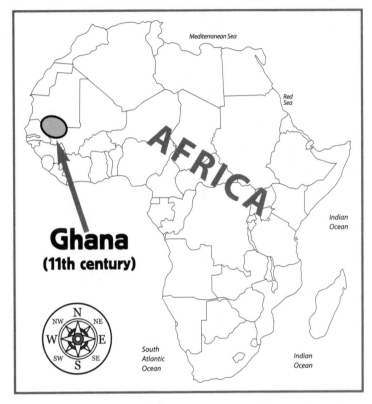

The region of Taghaza was in an open desert. Salt was so plentiful that blocks of it were used as building materials. Slaves forced to live in the region were responsible for cutting out 200-pound blocks of salt. Camels were loaded with the salt blocks and sent several hundred miles across the desert to the savanna. Many miners were blind from the severe sandstorms in the region. If the caravans returned late with fresh food, the slaves could starve to death!

Ghana's gold mines were located to the south. The mines were located in several places, but their exact locations were kept secret by the miners. Children and young girls who were small enough to go deep into the mines brought up gravel that was rinsed several times with water to separate the gold from the rocks.

Kings in Ghana did not control the gold mines, but they kept an eye on the supply to make sure they maintained wealth and power. They did this by taxing the gold as it made its way north: the king took the larger nuggets as "tax" and let the gold dust continue on northward. This kept the market from becoming too full of gold and making gold less valuable. During the mid-1000s, the king had enough gold to outfit the royal animals in gold ornaments!

AFRICA!

Empire of Mali

Other groups began attacking Ghana. By the 1300s the country of Mali had gained much of Ghana's power. In addition to gold and salt, Mali also traded copper, spices, ivory, ostrich feathers, and slaves. One of the things they traded for was fresh water, which they used to support dairy farms and crops of grain. Small farming villages lay beyond the larger cities. People in the villages were farmers who used short-handled hoes to grow crops such as beans, squash, melons, citrus fruits, and cereals such as sorghum and millet.

The Mali Empire reached its peak of power during the mid-1300s. The major city of Timbuktu was known for being a peaceful, fun-loving city. Parties with singing and dancing sometimes lasted all night. However, the good times came to an end in the late 1300s. At that time, pressures from other regions and problems involving the royal leaders led to Mali's decline.

If you look at the route the camels that carried the salt took, you will see that they left from Timbuktu heading east and they took a left turn to the north. Look at the map and see which landform would have made them take this route rather than heading straight to the north.

Write your answer here: _____

Songhai in Control

In the mid-1400s, Songhai was ruled by a powerful king named Sunni Ali. His goal was to extend his kingdom. In 1468, his army was able to capture Timbuktu, which meant the end of the Mali Empire. For more than 100 years, Songhai dominated the Upper Niger country and its trade northward across the desert from the market centers of Gao and Timbuktu.

Religion was somewhat important in Songhai. People were Muslims, but Songhai's main power was its military forces. Through the military, Songhai's king Ali was able to take over much of Mali. Until 1591, Songhai dominated West Africa. Then, the Moroccan army invaded and put the Songhai rule to an end.

Songhai, the last West African empire, was at its peak in 1450. Ghana reached its peak of power in 1250. Mali was at its peak in 1350.

Complete this timeline showing when Ghana, Mali, and Songhai were at their peak of power.

1250   1350   1450

_____   _____   _____

Put a check beside the people whom you think had the best life.

1. ____ farmer in Mali
2. ____ soldier from Songhai
3. ____ slave in a salt mine in Taghaza
4. ____ young girl working in gold mine in Ghana
5. ____ crew member on a Portuguese ship
6. ____ Resident of Timbuktu during the Mali Empire

After learning so much about the ancient empires of Mali, Ghana, and Songhai, you deserve a little fun. Here's a crossword puzzle that includes information you have already learned!

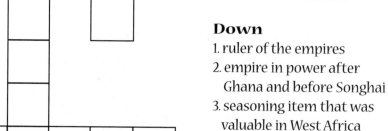

Across
3. the largest of the three empires
4. precious mineral mined in West Africa
5. people who worked in salt mines

Down
1. ruler of the empires
2. empire in power after Ghana and before Songhai
3. seasoning item that was valuable in West Africa
4. the first of the three empires

Section IV

History and Geography: Factors That Shaped Colonial America

Chapter 9

USI.5a—Describe the religious and economic events and conditions that led to the colonization of America. Correlates with USI.1a, USI.1c, and USI.1d.

The Colonial State of Mind

Colonies in America were established for religious and economic reasons. The first colonies were economic ventures. Roanoke Island was the first attempt at starting a colony in the New World. It eventually became known as the Lost Colony because all the settlers mysteriously disappeared. It was to be an economic experiment. The second try at colonization was Jamestown Settlement. In 1607, a group began a settlement that became the first permanent English settlement in North America. It was an economic venture by the Virginia Company.

The other purpose for starting colonies in the New World was religious freedom. People who wished to separate from the Church of England settled Plymouth colony. They wanted to avoid being punished for their religious beliefs. The Puritans settled the Massachusetts Bay Colony for the same reason. The Quakers settled Pennsylvania for religious reasons, too. They wanted the freedom to practice their faith without interference from the government.

Bad weather took the ship the Mayflower off course. The Mayflower was transporting Pilgrims. They realized that they were landing in an area different from what had been chartered to them, so they decided to create a document that spelled out some of the rules of their colony. This document, the Mayflower Compact, was written before the ship anchored on land. Most of the men aboard signed it. The Mayflower Compact was designed to maintain order in the colony. It was the first guide to self-government created in the colonies. The Mayflower Compact set up a General Court that made laws, imposed taxes, and elected leaders.

TRUE OR FALSE? The Mayflower Compact is an example of a primary source document. ❑ True ❑ False

The colony of Georgia was settled by people who had been in English debtor's prisons. Debtor's prisons were where people who couldn't (or wouldn't) pay their bills were sent! James Oglethorpe and some of his wealthy friends gave the debtors their start. A fresh start and a chance to gain economic independence were what the Georgia colonists hoped for.

Below is a list of the first settlements in the New World and the dates when they were settled. They are out of order.
Put them in chronological order by writing the letters beside them in the boxes on the timeline.

ⓐ Plymouth Colony, Massachusetts—1620

ⓑ Savannah, Georgia—1733

ⓒ Jamestown Settlement, Virginia—1607

ⓓ Pennsylvania—1681

ⓔ Massachusetts Bay Colony, Massachusetts—1630

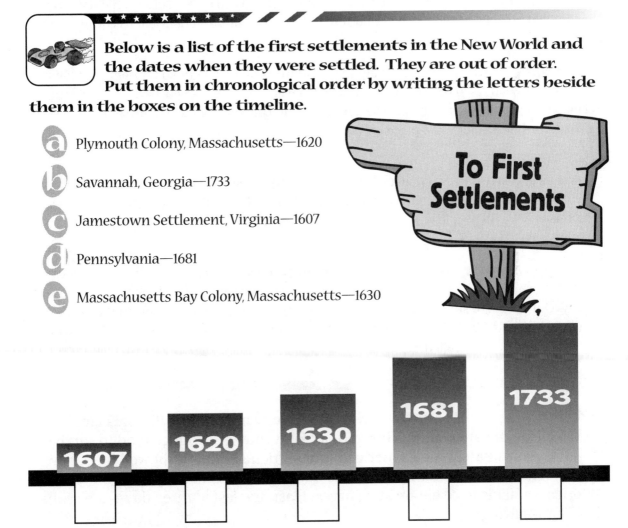

Here are some quotes from people who were on their way to becoming the first colonists.

Where Am I Going?

Write the destination of each colonist.

1. **I am a Pilgrim.** The Church of England has become too strict about making me follow their beliefs. When I heard fellow church members talking about a colony where we could practice our religion freely, I decided to go too. I am heading to
_____.

2. **I am following a leader** named William Penn to a new colony chartered by the king of England. We are Quakers hoping to have religious and political freedom in our new home. I am on my way to _____.

3. **I have a hard time** managing my finances. In fact, I got so far behind in paying my bills that I had to go to prison! Fortunately, a wealthy man named James Oglethorpe decided to give me and others like me a new start in the New World. We are hoping to start a prosperous new colony in a place called
_____.

4. **I am a member of a religious group** called the Puritans. We plan to start a colony that allows people to have political freedom, but we will strictly enforce our religious beliefs. All people who live in the colony must be Puritans. The colony we are forming is called _____.

5. **I am among some adventurous people** who are heading to the New World. Another group went before us, but they all disappeared. We call them the Lost Colony. Our goal is to start a profitable colony by growing some new crops that can't be grown in England. We think there will be lots of chances to make money in the New World. Our new colony will be called _____.

After they founded Plymouth Colony in 1620, the Pilgrims faced a long, hard winter. They did not know how to produce food to survive. Fortunately, their American Indian friend Squanto showed them how to grow a few crops. In 1621, they had a bountiful harvest. They invited the local American Indians to celebrate at a harvest feast that lasted three days! It was the first Thanksgiving!

Chapter 10

USI.5b—Compare and contrast life in the New England, Mid-Atlantic, and Southern colonies. Correlates with USI.1a, USI.1a, USI.1d, and USI.1f.

Colonial Regions, Alike and Different

Life in the colonies reflected the geographical features of the settlements. Climate and geography clearly distinguished the new colonies into three separate regions: New England, the Mid-Atlantic, and the South. The people of New England found hilly terrain with rocky soil and jagged coastlines. They enjoyed moderate summers and endured long, cold winters. The Appalachian Mountains and Boston Harbor were two of the main geological features.

In the Mid-Atlantic region, there were coastal lowlands with many harbors and bays, and wide, deep rivers. The Appalachian Mountains also ran through the region. Settlers there found rich farmland, which was easy to use because of the moderate climate.

The South was noted for several geographic regions, including the Appalachian Mountains, the Atlantic Coastal Plain, and the Piedmont. Good harbors and many rivers made it a favorable region. The warm, humid climate made it ideal for growing many crops.

Different Regions, Different Jobs

Geography and natural resources are important in deciding what is important to an area's economy. The plentiful coastline of New England made many people take jobs in the fishing industry. The shipbuilding industry also flourished...because the fishermen needed ships, of course. New England's numerous ports grew into cities. Ships left carrying goods, and ships arrived bringing in more goods. The area was a key to trade. Skilled craftsmen and shopkeepers also settled there.

The Mid-Atlantic's rich farmland was perfect for producing livestock. Grain to feed the livestock could also be easily grown in the Mid-Atlantic. Corn was often grown. A number of areas became major trading centers because of the coastal areas. Fishing was a key industry. Skilled and unskilled workers settled there.

In the South, agriculture was key to the economy. Both large plantations and small farms could be found throughout the region. Cash crops such as tobacco, rice, and indigo were important. Wood products were important to the economy. Much of the work—especially the hard, hot work in the fields—was done by slaves.

Below are some sentences that apply to people who lived in the colonies. On the line beside each, write where the person would most likely have settled. Use N for New England, M for Mid-Atlantic, and S for the South.

1. _____ I raised dairy cattle and hogs for a living. My farm was on the banks of a large river.

2. _____ I learned to build ships in England. When people started going to the colonies, I thought I could come too and make a good living as a shipbuilder.

3. _____ My trade was as a fisherman. I knew the New England region was good for fishing, but it was just too cold there for me. I ended up settling in this region instead.

4. _____ I was taken from my family in Africa and forced to make a long journey deep within a hot, smelly ship. Now I do hard work picking tobacco on a plantation.

Indigo is a plant used to make blue dye for cloth. This dye was popular in England during the colonial period.

Use this map to help you learn about how the climate, natural resources, and geography of the area led to specific trades and industries becoming common in that region.

① Draw an ear of corn beside the region where grain was often grown.

② Draw a plantation house beside the region where homes of this type were most common.

③ Draw a boat beside the region where shipbuilding was most likely to take place.

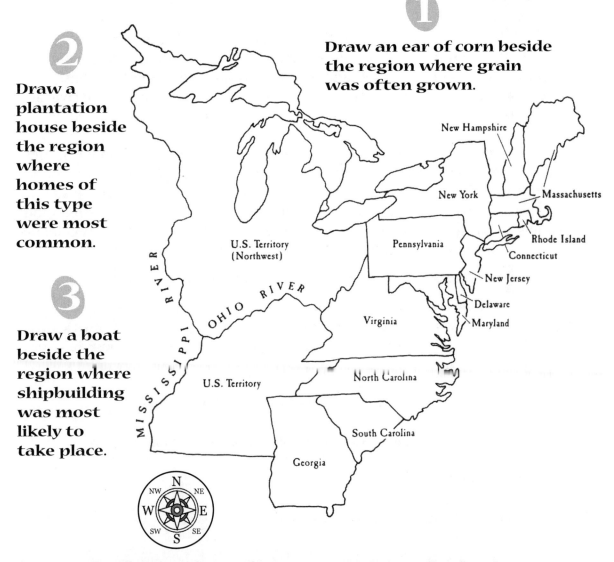

For Society's Sake

The three colonial regions had different social relationships. Groups of people settled in New England in villages and cities. Most settlements in New England were formed by people seeking the freedom to worship without government interference. The church was the center of social life. New Englanders were involved in political and civic affairs. They discussed city business at town meetings.

In the Mid-Atlantic region, villages and cities were also common, but people were more diverse. Colonists from other countries, as well as England, settled here. They brought different religions, traditions, and cultures, leading to more varied settlements. Most of the civic and political involvement took place in market towns where more people lived.

People were scattered in small groups in the South. Many lived on farms, both large and small. They grew and gathered food, made their own cloth and clothing, and took care of themselves without interacting much with others. Slaves and indentured servants were common in the South. There were few cities or schools. The Church of England was the main church and a center of social life. The South was divided into counties—centers of political and civic life.

Look at the following documents and decide if they are primary source documents or secondary source documents. Write a P beside those that are primary and an S beside the ones that are secondary.

1. ____ The Rev. Edward Smith's sermon on loving thy neighbor as thyself

2. ____ A college professor's paper about colonial life in the Mid-Atlantic region

3. ____ The minutes from a town meeting of a New England village

4. ____ A Southern plantation owner's records of crops and yields

Look at these pictures and photographs and determine which region they best describe. In the space provided, write New England, Mid-Atlantic, or Southern.

long, cold winters	land divided into counties	Boston Harbor
	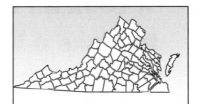	
_____	_____	_____

plantations	livestock farms	mountain range in all three regions

_____	_____	_____

rich farmland	A humid climate	colonized for religious reasons

_____	_____	_____

Chapter 11

USI.5c—*Describe colonial life in America from multiple perspectives. Correlates with USI.1d.*

It Took All Kinds to Make a World

The colonies were made up of groups of people whose lives were different based on their social position. Colonial Americans could be divided into six groups:

- slaves
- farmers
- artisans
- women
- large landowners
- indentured servants

artisan: a person skilled in an art form; a craftsperson. Weavers, glassblowers, and carpenters are all artisans.

indentured servant: a person who is legally bound by a contract to work for another as a servant or apprentice for a certain length of time

Wealth and gender were the two main factors in deciding a person's lot in life. Men usually had more privileges than women, and wealthy people had more opportunities to become educated and enjoy social affairs.

The wealthiest people in colonial America were usually those who owned large amounts of land. **Plantation owners** mainly lived in the South. The plantations they owned produced crops such as tobacco, sugar, and indigo. They didn't have to do much work themselves because they had indentured servants and slaves to do the work for them. Large landowners were often able to obtain an education, and they enjoyed a rich social culture that included music, dancing, and parties.

Colonial **farmers** were not as wealthy as the large landowners. They and their families did the work themselves. Location decided what was produced. In New England, they raised livestock such as sheep. In the Mid-Atlantic, they grew tobacco and grains, and in the South they grew rice, indigo, cotton, and tobacco.

Artisans settled in all areas of the colonies. In both towns and on plantations, they worked as craftsmen. They lived in small villages and cities. In some cases, women were artisans.

Women served in domestic roles, such as caretakers, house workers, and homemakers. They had no political rights and were not allowed to vote. Women had little chance of getting an education.

Another group of colonists were **indentured servants**. They wanted to go to the colonies so badly that they signed away years of their lives. They couldn't afford to pay for a trip, so they would find a ship captain to transport them to America. The ship captain would take them to the colonies, where he would contract with a merchant, artisan, or plantation owner to employ the person as an indentured servant for a set amount of time—usually three to five years. Once the time was up, the indentured servant was free to start a life of his own.

Being an indentured servant was better than being a slave. The contract was binding. If the indentured servant ran away, he could be brought back and beaten and have the time of service lengthened. The work was often long and hard. However, indentured servants knew that they would eventually be free.

Slaves had the hardest lives. They didn't choose to come to the colonies, but were captured in their native Africa. Captured Africans were sold to slave traders, who chained the Africans and threw them into the dark, hot holds of ships. Many became sick and died. It was a sad situation to become a slave. Once someone was enslaved, he or she would be a slave all his life. Even children born to slaves would be slaves forever. Slaves were not seen as human beings—but as property. They had no rights and were often mistreated.

Now that you have an idea of what life was like in colonial America, try this activity to see what you have learned. Below is a matching exercise. Look at the types of people who lived in the colonies. Read the quote and match it to the type of person who most likely said it.

_____ 1. Artisan   _____ 3. Colonial woman   _____ 5. Farmer

_____ 2. Indentured servant _____ 4. Plantation owner _____ 6. Slave

A. I hope the rain holds off for a few days. I have the seeds I need to plant a few acres of beans. My sons work hard and help me a great deal.

B. I look forward to day's end when I can come in off the fields and rest for a few hours. My back hurts from bending over to pick cotton. I miss the sights and sounds of my homeland in Africa, but mostly I miss my freedom.

C. A new shipment of mahogany wood just came in from Africa. I am very excited because I have been working on a design for a chair that would be beautiful if it were made from mahogany.

D. Today will be a busy day! I must make the bread and do some mending. The linens have to be washed and hung to dry. That means a day of ironing! There is a town meeting tomorrow, but it doesn't matter because I cannot vote anyway.

E. The trip to America was a long one. I was excited and scared. I agreed to work five years in a candle-maker's shop. I have thought about running away, but if I were caught, I'd have to keep working at this job even longer. In a little more than three years I can do whatever I want!

F. It won't be long before the tobacco is ready to harvest. We should have a good yield this year. Then we can hold a harvest ball! I am very excited because there is a new dance from France that people are learning. In the spring I think I will visit France myself!

Chapter 12

USI.5d—Identify the political and economic relationships between the colonies and England. Correlates with USI.1d and USI.1f.

Trying To Get Out of Control!

When the colonies were first being founded, support from England was accepted. England was far enough away not to hover, but was still reachable. After a while, though, England began to expand its control over the colonies more and more.

The main way England controlled the colonies was by economic means. England strictly controlled the colonies' trade. It took some time before the colonies were settled enough to produce goods they could trade, but once they did, England made laws saying the colonies could sell their goods only to England. Of course, England also decided the price that would be paid. The colonies couldn't buy goods from other countries, either!

England believed it needed money from the colonists. In the mid-1700s, England was involved in the French and Indian War. After the war was over, England was almost broke. England also had acquired a great deal of new territory from France by winning the war, and the British felt the colonies should help build up England's bank account. England began taxing the colonists. In addition to raising funds, the taxes gave England even more control over the colonies. The only method that the colonies had of flexing their own economic strength was by trading raw materials for goods.

England passed one law called the Molasses Act, which prevented the American colonists from buying molasses from French colonies in the West Indies. The American colonists managed to smuggle it in, though!

Read these quotes. If they were said by American colonists, write an A. If they were said by a member of the English government, write an E.

1. _____ I can see that you are ordering more tea. I will have to make you pay a tax on it.

2. _____ I am sending you fine cured tobacco. I need some tea and some linen cloth.

3. _____ I will need you to pay the tax on the tea and linen in advance.

4. _____ The law says we can't buy West Indies molasses, but we need it for our baking!

Politically Correct?

The American colonies and England also had political relationships. The colonists had to obey English laws. English governors enforced the laws. The king of England or his proprietor appointed the colonial governors. The colonial governors monitored laws created by the colonial law-making bodies of legislators.

proprietor: A person who owned or operated a colony

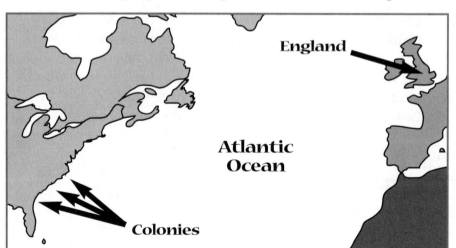

Look at the map shown here.

3. What is the main body of water separating England from the colonies?

_____

Section V

History and Civics: Causes and Results of the American Revolution

Chapter 13

USI.6a—*Identify the issues that led to the American Revolution. Correlates with USI.1b, USI.1c and USI.1d.*

Knowing When to Say No!

As England expanded its control over the American colonies, many colonists became dissatisfied and rebellious. England took several steps to increase control over the Colonies. For example, England imposed taxes, such as the Stamp Act. The purpose of the Stamp Act was to raise the revenue needed to pay for the cost of the French and Indian War, which had taken place in the Colonies. This had been a very expensive war for England.

ENGLAND RULES! Taxes were also levied against the American colonies to help finance the cost of maintaining the English troops who were stationed in the colonies. England desired to remain a world power.

Put the following events in the order in which they occurred.

_____ Colonies help maintain English troops by paying taxes.

_____ The French and Indian War takes place in the Colonies.

_____ The Stamp Act is passed.

_____ Colonists become dissatisfied and rebellious.

Enough is Enough!

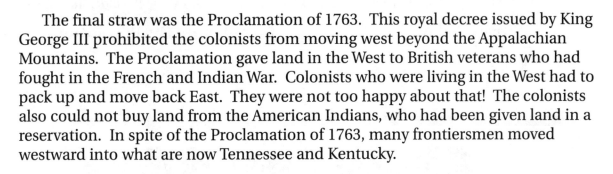

Finally the colonies had had enough. They opposed being taxed by England—especially since they were getting taxed without having the chance to have any say about it! The colonies had no representation in Parliament. Parliament is the governing body of England. Many colonists resented the power of the colonial governors and how England wanted strict control over the colonial legislatures, which were trying to make laws to help and protect the colonists.

The final straw was the Proclamation of 1763. This royal decree issued by King George III prohibited the colonists from moving west beyond the Appalachian Mountains. The Proclamation gave land in the West to British veterans who had fought in the French and Indian War. Colonists who were living in the West had to pack up and move back East. They were not too happy about that! The colonists also could not buy land from the American Indians, who had been given land in a reservation. In spite of the Proclamation of 1763, many frontiersmen moved westward into what are now Tennessee and Kentucky.

As England tried to control the colonies more and more, the colonists became dissatisfied and rebellious.

 Pretend you are a colonist. You are asked your opinion about these matters. Put a checkmark to indicate how you feel.

1. Pay tax, but have no say-so? __YES __NO

2. Pay more than our fair share for war debt? __YES __NO

3. Be ruled by faraway England? __YES __NO

4. Establish local assemblies in the colonies? __YES __NO

5. Fight for our independence? __YES __NO

Answer the following questions.

1. In the mid-1700s, England, France, and Spain were considered world powers. What country is a world power today?
_____ _____ _____ _____

2. In the mid-1700s, England taxed the American colonists to help finance the cost of the French and Indian War. Today, how does the American government come up with the money to pay for a war? _____

3. What is a difference between taxes today and those before the Revolutionary War?

Taxes Today	Taxes before the Revolution
_____	_____
_____	_____

Chapter 14

USI.6b—Identify how political ideas shaped the revolutionary movement in America and led to the Declaration of Independence. Correlates with USI.1a, USI.1b, USI.1d, and USI.1h.

Strong New Voices Emerging

New political ideas led to a desire for independence and democratic government in the American colonies. Nearly 80 years before the colonists were beginning to think about a revolution against England, an English philosopher was writing books that would influence the patriots. The philosopher's name was John Locke. Many colonists read and firmly believed Locke's ideas.

 philosophy: the study of the meaning of life and the problems of right and wrong

In the late 1600s, Locke wrote a book called *Two Treatises of Government.* He wrote that people have natural rights. Natural rights are those that cannot be taken away. To Locke, these included the right to life, liberty, and property. By liberty, Locke meant political equality.

Locke also expressed the idea that government is created to protect the rights of people. Government has only the powers the people agree to give it. These powers are limited and specific. If the government cannot protect the citizens' rights, the citizens have the right to choose new leaders who will do the job they are supposed to do.

TRUE OR FALSE? John Locke's book *Two Treatises of Government* is an example of a primary source document.

❏ **True**   ❏ **False**

Here is an excerpt from John Locke's book:

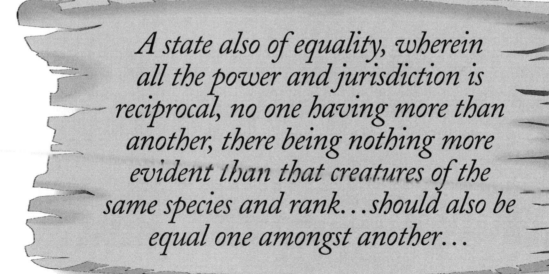

A state also of equality, wherein all the power and jurisdiction is reciprocal, no one having more than another, there being nothing more evident than that creatures of the same species and rank...should also be equal one amongst another...

What did Locke mean when he used the word "equality"? _____

_____

The Ideas Live On!

John Locke's ideas went on to influence Thomas Jefferson when he was writing the Declaration of Independence. The Declaration of Independence proclaimed the colonies' independence from England. It stated that people have natural (inherent) rights to life, liberty, and the pursuit of happiness.

In Thomas Jefferson's words, people have "certain unalienable rights." These are rights that cannot be taken away.

In the paragraph that begins, "In Thomas Jefferson's…," what words are from a primary source document?

_____

In the following paragraphs, can you find another example of text from a primary source document?

_____

Another key philosophy in the Declaration of Independence, just like in Locke's writings, is that people establish government to protect their rights to "life, liberty, and the pursuit of happiness." The government that people establish gets its power from the people, and they have a right and a duty to change a government that violates their rights.

Locke

As an Englishman, Locke's experience included living in a monarchy with a king. However, Locke supported throwing out a ruler if he was not doing a good job. The ruler had to take care of the people in the kingdom and make sure that their rights were preserved. In fact, John Locke's friend, William of Orange, replaced King James II.

Jefferson wrote in the Declaration of Independence that when government stops protecting the people it was made to protect, the people must change or completely get rid of the government.

In the Declaration of Independence, Jefferson listed many reasons why the colonists were tired of being governed by the British.

Here are some phrases from the Declaration of Independence. Below them are more modern ways of saying what Jefferson said. Write the letter of the more modern interpretation that best matches Jefferson's original writing.

1. ____ He has erected a multitude of New Offices, and sent hither swarms of Officers to harass our people, and eat out their substance.

2. ____ He has forbidden his Governors to pass Laws of immediate and pressing importance…

3. ____ For cutting off our Trade with other parts of the world.

4. ____ For imposing taxes on us without our consent.

5. ____ For Quartering large bodies of armed troops among us…

A. We cannot trade with other countries.

B. The king has made many people his employees and has sent them to America, where they bother the colonists and eat the colonists' food.

C. The king has sent many soldiers to the colonies and made them live in the home of the colonists.

D. The king's governors cannot pass laws quickly enough to prevent problems.

E. The king taxes the colonists without the colonists having any say about it.

Today, people can voice their opinions about government at election time. They can vote for people they believe would be good at governing and they can vote on whether or not taxes will be put into effect.

Look at the table below. Make a √ under the date describing what government was like in 1760 or today. Keep in mind that the Declaration of Independence was written to say why the colonists were tired of being governed by England.

EVENT	1760	TODAY
The king appointed governors		
People vote on taxes		
People couldn't voice their opinion about government		
People can vote to have bad leaders removed		

 Who said it? These quotes are from John Locke's writing and Thomas Jefferson's writing. Beside each, write the writers' initials.

1. ____ People have "certain unalienable rights"—life, liberty, and the pursuit of happiness.

2. ____ People have natural rights to life, liberty, and property.

Jefferson

"Goochland (now Albemarle County), Virginia was my home. I was born there in 1743. I've been a lawyer, statesman, political theorist, musician, planter, architect, and archaeologist, and wrote the first draft of the Declaration of Independence. In 1801, I became America's third president. I enlarged America through the Louisiana Purchase, and sent Meriwether Lewis and William Clark on their famous expedition. However, I guess I'm most proud of founding the University of Virginia. An education is essential, you know. My name is THOMAS JEFFERSON."

Chapter 15

USI.6c—Describe key events and the roles of key individuals in the American Revolution. Correlates with USI.1a, USI.1c, USI.1d, USI.1f, and USI.1h.

Join the Revolution!

Many individuals played important roles in shaping events of the American Revolution. Here are some of the key people involved and the role they had:

King George III—British king during the Revolutionary era

Lord Cornwallis—British general who surrendered at Yorktown

John Adams—a main supporter of independence

George Washington—commander of the Continental Army

Thomas Jefferson—main author of the *Declaration of Independence*

Patrick Henry—outspoken member of the House of Burgesses; inspired the patriots with his stirring *speech*, "Give me liberty or give me death!"

Benjamin Franklin—prominent member of the Continental Congress who helped frame the *Declaration of Independence*

Thomas Paine—journalist who was the author of *Common Sense*

 Hidden in the list of important Revolutionary figures above are examples of primary source documents. List at least two.

_____   _____

On March 23, 1775, Virginia's second revolutionary convention met in Richmond to discuss if the colonies should enter a war against the British. One member of the House of Burgesses gave a fiery speech.

Patrick Henry looked at his fellow patriots and said all they had done to keep peace and stay out of war against England had been for nothing.

"There is no longer any room for hope," he declared. "If we wish to be free… we must fight! Gentlemen may cry, 'Peace! Peace!' but there is no peace. The war has actually begun! Is life so dear, or peace so sweet, as to be purchased at the price of chains and slavery? Forbid it, Almighty God! I know not what course others may take, but as for me, give me liberty, or give me death!"

1. Are Patrick Henry's actual words an example of a primary or secondary source document? _____

2. In saying, "Give me liberty, or give me death," what did Patrick Henry mean?

_____

_____

_____

In Patrick Henry's speech, he speaks of knowing not what course others may take. What did he mean by the word "course"? Use a dictionary to help you.

_____

_____

Voice of a Poet

During the Revolutionary period, Phillis Wheatley became known as a popular writer. She wrote poems and plays supporting American independence. She was a most unusual person because not only was she a woman writer, but she was also a former slave!

Phillis came from Africa aboard a slave ship, and when John Wheatley brought her home, she did not know how to speak English. The family liked her very much and allowed her to be more a part of the family than slaves were usually allowed. The Wheatleys taught Phillis to read and write, and she wrote poems about subjects that interested her.

Phillis' most famous poem was "On the Death of the Reverend George Whitefield." The Reverend Whitefield was a popular minister of the time, and many people bought the poem. Her work also became well liked in England.

The Wheatleys gave Phillis her freedom, and when John Wheatley died, she received an inheritance. She bought a house and married a man named John Peters. He did not seem to appreciate her talent and quickly spent all the money she had been left. The couple had three children, but two died as babies. She and her third baby died within a few hours of each other on December 5, 1784. Phillis Wheatley was only 31 years old.

Here are a few lines from one of Phillis Wheatley's poems, "On being brought from Africa to America":

"'Twas mercy brought me from my Pagan land,
Taught my benighted soul to understand
That there's a God, and there's a Saviour too:
Once I redemption neither sought nor knew."

Can you put the lines from Phillis Wheatley's poem into your own words? You may need a dictionary for some of the more difficult words.

Is your interpretation of Phillis Wheatley's poem a primary or secondary source document?

_____

 Look at the map below and draw a crown in the country where King George III lived during the Revolutionary War. Draw a star on the area where patriots from the American colonies lived.

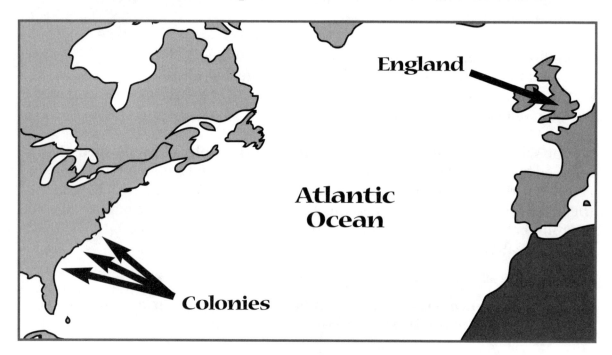

In 1763, Boston was a major city. It had more that 42 streets and 3,000 houses. There were hundreds of shops where craftsmen made everything from chairs to anchors. People dressed in the clothing style of the British. One visitor said Boston was more like "an English town than any in America."

On the Way to Rebellion

When England began exerting more control over the colonists, they became more and more angry. In Boston in the late 1760s, tempers began to flare strongly after the British began taxing the colonists more. The Stamp Tax, Molasses Tax, and Tea Tax are examples. When the taxes were issued, the people of Boston rioted. British troops were sent to maintain order.

The Boston citizens resented having the British troops in the city. They teased and taunted the soldiers. On March 5, 1770, they kept bombarding the soldiers with snowballs as well as yelling at them and calling them names like "lobster backs." Finally, the soldiers had had enough! They fired their guns into a crowd. When the conflict was over, five people were dead and six were injured. This event came to be known as the Boston Massacre.

This event gave the independence-seeking colonists more reason to want to rebel against England. In 1773, the British imposed the Tea Tax. On December 16th of that year, a group of men who called themselves the Sons of Liberty disguised themselves as Indians. They boarded a ship carrying tea and dumped 342 chests of tea into Boston Harbor. This act of rebellion encouraged others to join the battle against England.

British soldiers wore red coats for a reason. When a soldier was hit by a musket ball, the red coat made it hard for others to know he was bleeding. This stopped soldiers from getting scared and running away!

Put the following events in order in which they took place. Label them 1, 2, and 3.

___ Boston Tea Party   ___ Tea Tax   ___ Boston Massacre

Jack-of-all-Trades, Master of Many

One of the best-known figures in American history is Benjamin Franklin. Franklin invented many useful items such as bifocal glasses and the Franklin stove. He helped to improve the city of Philadelphia by starting a public library and a volunteer fire department.

At first, Benjamin Franklin did not favor independence for the colonies. He and many friends considered England the most free nation in the world and a wonderful sponsor for the colonies.

Franklin's opinion of England changed, though, when he was there on business in 1757. A British lord told him that Americans better think again if they thought the King's instructions to his governors were not laws that applied to the colonists. The British government also unjustly accused Franklin of trying to cheat Britain. It was almost like England was daring him to become a patriot! Franklin became more and more dissatisfied with British government.

From 1765 to 1775, Franklin was the leading American spokesman in England. He knew more about America than anyone in England, and more about England than anyone else in America. The English government disappointed him more and more. The final blow was the Tea Act of 1773. He wrote an essay, "Rules by Which a Great Empire May Be Reduced to a Small One," to show the British how they were pushing the Americans to start a revolution.

At the age of 70, he became a revolutionary. He was a prominent member of the Second Continental Congress and helped write the framework for the Declaration of Independence. When he died at the age of 84, Benjamin Franklin was remembered as a leader of the founding fathers of the United States.

The passage about Benjamin Franklin mentions four primary source documents. Can you list at least two?

_____   _____

On the Road to War

Paul Revere was a well-known patriot of the Revolutionary War. He is best known for his midnight ride to warn the colonists of the arrival of the British troops.

Paul Revere became involved in supporting the colonies' fight for independence from England at the end of the Seven Years' War in 1763. He was a member of the Sons of Liberty who didn't like the way England treated the colonies. He also participated in the Boston Tea Party, when he and Samuel Adams led a group of patriots disguised as Indians. They threw barrels of tea into Boston Harbor to protest the English taxes on tea.

Revere was known for his beautiful work as a silversmith. His work was some of the finest produced during the colonial period. Revere also designed and printed the first money used in the colonies, and he made the first official seal for the colonies. During the Revolutionary War, he served as a messenger and also made gunpowder. With his experience in metalworking, he was able to cast cannons for the American Army.

After the war, he continued to work with metals and learned how to roll copper sheets. These sheets were used for the hulls of ships and for buildings. He made the copper sheets that were used to cover the dome of the Massachusetts State House.

Imagine you are Paul Revere. Write your feelings about the following topics:

1. the Boston Massacre: _____

2. the Boston Tea Party: _____

3. the ride to warn the colonists the British were coming: _____

_____

A Matter of Common Sense

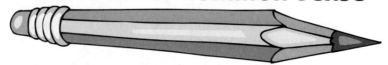

Thomas Paine, a journalist during the colonial period, at first supported keeping a good relationship with England. However, after the battles of Lexington and Concord in April 1775, he changed his mind. He wrote a pamphlet titled *Common Sense*. It was based on John Locke's philosophies that people have natural rights such as life and liberty, and that revolution may be necessary to bring happiness. Many people read *Common Sense* and were influenced by Paine. The Continental Congress also drew from it.

Common Sense didn't just say that the colonies should reject British rule, but more importantly, that the colonies should adopt a new system of government. Paine believed that the American Revolution was a war in which people were trying to keep their natural rights, and not just an effort to change government. *Common Sense* prompted people to discuss issues such as English constitutional ideas, the beginnings of government, and independence.

In *Common Sense*, Paine pointed out that government is a human wish to restrain lawlessness, but having to have government shows that things are not going so well. He wrote that people who create government can corrupt it. Paine believed that the simpler government is, the easier it is for people to see its weaknesses. A monarchy like Britain's, he said, had done away with the good qualities of government and had made the people think government is not good. America had to get away from this and be independent in order to survive!

QUESTION: During the American Revolution, Thomas Paine wrote, "These are the times that try men's souls." What do you think he meant by this?

_____

_____

_____

Truly Declaring Independence

Common Sense caught the attention of many people during the American Revolution. Thomas Jefferson was one person who read and was impressed by it. In fact, *Common Sense* prepared people for ideas that Jefferson would use in the Declaration of Independence—ideas such as "life, liberty, and the pursuit of happiness."

Thomas Jefferson was a Virginian who served in the House of Burgesses, as his father had before him. Jefferson's father died when Jefferson was only 14 years old, leaving him to run a large farm with 30 slaves. In 1760 he enrolled at the College of William and Mary in Williamsburg. He graduated two years later at the age of 19. After getting his degree, Jefferson studied law and became a lawyer in 1767. His great skill was in writing. Other burgesses often asked Thomas Jefferson to write laws and resolutions for them.

In 1776, Thomas Jefferson was 33 years old. He was a member of the Continental Congress in Philadelphia. The Congress decided a written document would show England why the colonies wanted to be a separate country. Many members of the Congress were more experienced leaders, but Thomas Jefferson was known for his ability as a writer. He was asked to write the document to give to England. It was called the Declaration of Independence. It took Jefferson only a few days to write the Declaration.

Thomas Jefferson went on to do many more great things for the new nation, including serving as president and making one of the best land-buying deals ever!

Based on what you have read about conventions, answer this question.

A convention is:

____ A. a formal meeting or assembly   ____ B. an informal gathering

A Leader of Men

George Washington was born to a Virginia family who owned land, but was not exceptionally prosperous. His father died when George was a child. George dreamed of an adventurous life at sea, but his mother begged him to stay with her and manage the family estate. He also wasn't able to go to England and get a formal education, as sons of planters often did in the colonial period. Still, George was very intelligent. He was tall and strong and known for his skills as a horseman.

When George was a teenager, he was invited to go on a surveying trip. At age 17 he became the surveyor of Culpeper County, Virginia. This job would help him in the future because he learned a great deal about land formations and Indian trails and the general lay of the land.

At age 21, Washington was appointed a major in England's army. He fought in the French and Indian War and learned the techniques of the British army and the strength of the French army. In 1755, he was picked to command the entire Virginia militia.

George served in the House of Burgesses, where he earned the reputation of being able to help people with different opinions work out their differences peacefully. Washington did agree with the colonists who were becoming irritated by the unfairness of England's government. In 1774, Washington served as a Virginia delegate to the First Constitutional Congress in Philadelphia. In 1775, at the Second Constitutional Congress, he was elected general of the Continental Army.

The challenges were great. The Continental Army was formed of mainly untrained volunteers who even fought among themselves. They didn't have many supplies or proper uniforms. Yet, George Washington organized them and inspired them. He led them to a couple of key victories, and the rag-tag army collected a surrender from a great world power in October 1781.

George Washington served in both the British and Continental (colonial) armies.

Look at the dates below and determine if he was a supporter or an opponent of the British army. Make a √ if he supported it or an X if he opposed it.

DATE	SUPPORTED/OPPOSED BRITISH
1757	
1778	

Mapping History

Following the 1770 Boston Massacre, where Boston colonists were shot after teasing British soldiers, the Boston Tea Party took place. The "party" was a group of patriots led by Paul Revere and Samuel Adams. They threw hundreds of chests of tea into Boston Harbor to protest tea taxes imposed by the British government. Tired of being badgered by the British government, delegates from all the colonies, except Georgia, met in Philadelphia at the First Continental Congress in 1774. The purpose of the congress was to discuss the problems the colonies were having with England and to promote independence.

King George III had said the colonies would not become independent without a fight, and in 1775, the colonists gave the Redcoats just that. The first armed conflict of the American Revolution took place at Lexington and Concord on April 19.

After several battles, the Second Continental Congress met. Participants listed the reasons why the American colonies should be independent, and these were written up in a document called the Declaration of Independence. It was approved on July 4, 1776.

The turning point of the Revolution came in the fall of 1777 when the American troops were able to defeat the British at the battle of Saratoga in New York. This victory convinced France that the American colonies stood a good chance of becoming independent, so the French supported the colonies. They viewed anyone who was against Britain as a friend.

Finally, in 1781, the Continental Army defeated Lord Cornwallis and his troops at Yorktown, Virginia. The British had had enough of the war! In November 1781, England surrendered to George Washington in Yorktown. America had won its independence!

In 1783, the Treaty of Paris was signed in Paris, France. With this, the kingdom of England finally officially recognized the independence of the 13 states of America.

Here is a timeline showing some of the key dates leading up to the American Revolution and some of the key events of the war:

- **1770**—Boston Massacre in Boston
- **1773**—Boston Tea Party in Boston Harbor
- **1774**—First Continental Congress in Philadelphia
- **1775**—battle at Lexington and Concord
- **1776**—Declaration of Independence in Philadelphia
- **1777**—Battle of Saratoga in New York
- **1781**—British surrender in Virginia
- **1783**—Treaty of Paris in Paris, France

Using the information on the timeline, write a date in each of the boxes on this map to show when a specific event took place. One is done for you.

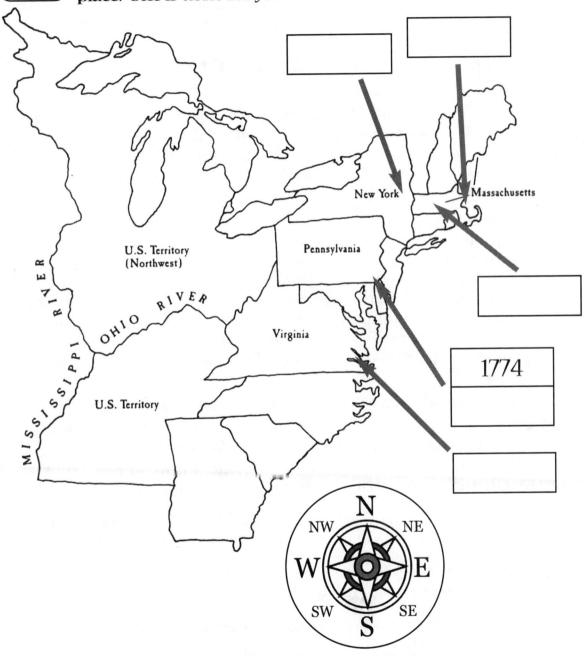

Chapter 16

Standard US1.6d—Explain the reasons why the colonies were able to defeat the British. Correlates with USI.1d and USI.1f.

Recipe for Victory!

How could it happen? A country with no real financial standing and no military power could defeat the richest, most powerful country in the world? It didn't seem likely, but the American colonies managed to pull off such an amazing achievement by defeating England. The Americans had several advantages that helped them win the Revolutionary War.

Sheer determination may have been one of the key ingredients in the recipe for victory, but other factors were included, too. The colonists wanted to defend having land of their own, and they also wanted to fight to be able to keep their strong beliefs. American colonists had the advantage of strong leadership. When the leaders of France and Spain, two other world powers, saw that the colonists were defeating the giant British empire, they gave their support to the colonists. Combined, these factors gave the Americans what they needed to defeat the British in the Revolutionary War. It may have been an unlikely recipe for victory, but it worked.

Look at these sentences and determine who said them. Put a C by those statements made by colonists, an L by those said by strong colonial leaders and an E by those said by European countries, including France, Spain, and England.

1. ____ It is unbelievable that the Americans colonies are beating the British Army. Their army doesn't have any money or training. We must give them financial support!

2. ____ We cannot let England control every aspect of our lives. We must inspire our army and convince the troops they can defeat the redcoats!

3. ____ The king of England better think again if he thinks he's sending in his lobster backs to take my land away from me!

Here is a map showing the colonies and Europe. Locate Spain and France in Europe and put an S on each of these countries. The S stands for supporters of the colonies. Put an E on England. The E can stand for England, but in this case, E for enemy may be more correct. Put a V on the colonies because they were the victors in the Revolutionary War.

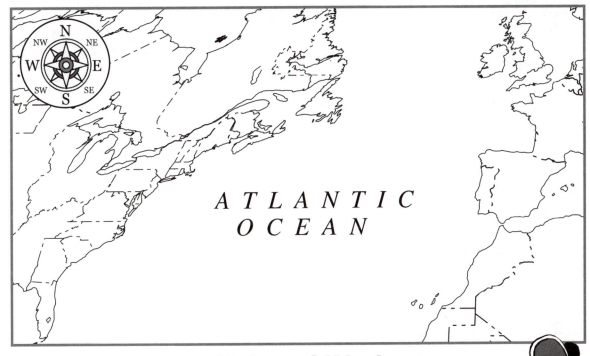

Rules of War!

The British army was used to fighting wars in an orderly fashion. Soldiers lined up and marched into battle. Some members of the Continental Army, including commander General George Washington, had seen how the Indians fought, by hiding and jumping out from trees and boulders in surprise attacks.

Why would the colonists have had an advantage in all the battles taking place on their land?

_____

_____

Choose the settings below that would not have been likely battle sites during the American Revolution.

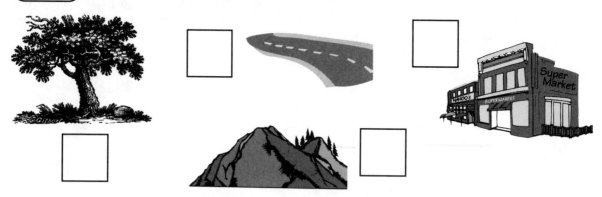

Do you think that America's strong desire for freedom helped the colonists win the Revolutionary War? If your answer is yes, how did it help them?

_____
_____
_____
_____
_____
_____
_____
_____
_____
_____
_____
_____
_____
_____

Section VI

History and Civics:
Challenges of a New Nation

Chapter 17

Standard USI.7a—Identify the weaknesses of the government established by the Articles of Confederation. Correlates with USI.1a, USI.1d, and USI.1f.

A Place to Start

During the American Revolution, the men who held leadership positions realized that independence would bring about the need for a form of government. They began forming the Articles of Confederation. It was a constitution to establish the powers of a new national government. It was the first constitution of the United States.

At first the Articles were written with a stronger central government in mind. Many states opposed this, because, on one hand, people were more loyal to the area they came from than to the new nation as a whole. Besides, hadn't the colonies just fought a war to protest the powerful central government of England? Small farmers and workers generally had this point of view.

On the other hand, some patriots, larger landowners, and merchants thought a strong national government would be better. They thought a strong national government would protect their property rights and keep trading practices fair.

The Articles of Confederation went into effect on March 1, 1781. They provided for a weak national government.

Look at the people listed here. Decide if they favored the original or the revised edition of the Articles of the Confederation. Write an O beside those who favored the original and an R beside those people who favored the revised version.

1. ____ farmer on a dairy farm in Maryland

2. ____ owner of a large tobacco plantation in Virginia

3. ____ shipbuilder in Massachusetts

States with set boundaries, such as Pennsylvania and Maryland, would not have any way to claim lands in the west. They wanted Congress to make the states with claims to land in the west, such as New York, Virginia, and Connecticut, give up the land. Of course, those states did not want to give up the land. Maryland would not agree to ratify the Articles of Confederation unless the western lands were put under the control of Congress. Finally, the Articles of Confederation could go into effect.

Look at this map, which shows what the United States looked like in 1787.

Color Maryland and Pennsylvania the same color.

Color New York, Virginia and Connecticut the same color.

What was the last state to ratify the Articles of Confederation? Put a √ on it.

 ratify: to give formal approval to something so that it can become valid

More Power to the States

By providing a weak national government, the Articles of Confederation gave the individual states the most authority over their own affairs. The Articles specified that any power not expressly given to Congress belonged to the states. Congress' authority was limited. Congress could declare war and peace, but it could not levy taxes. Congress could establish and command an army and navy. Congress could handle foreign affairs. Congress could make laws, but could not force the states to comply with them. Congress could not regulate commerce among the states, and it couldn't establish a set commercial policy for the nation.

The Articles of Confederation also gave each state only one vote, regardless of how many people lived there. This was meant to make each state equal, but many people had felt representation should be proportional, based on the number of people who lived in the state. This meant that states with more people would have more votes.

Another weakness in the Articles of Confederation that soon became obvious was the fact that it provided for no executive or judicial branch, only a legislative branch. The legislative branch could make laws but could not force the states to obey them. The Articles of Confederation were a good start, but changes would have to be made.

 In the table below list what the Congress of 1788 could and could not do based on the Articles of Confederation rules.

1788 CONGRESS

COULD	COULD NOT
Start an army	Levy taxes

Match the following quotes from the Articles of Confederation with their more modern translation.

1. …the people of each State shall free ingress and regress to and from any other State…

2. No state shall engage in any war without the consent of the United States in Congress assembled…

3. If any person guilty of, or charged with, treason, felony, or other high misdemeanor in any State, shall flee from justice, and be found in any of the United States, he shall, upon demand of the Governor or executive power of the State from which he fled, be delivered up and removed to the State having jurisdiction of his offense.

4. In determining questions in the United States in Congress assembled, each State shall have one vote.

____ States cannot declare war without an approval from Congress.

____ Each state has one vote in Congress.

____ People can come and go between their states and other states.

____ If someone charged with a crime flees a state, the governor of that state can demand that the person be brought back to the state where the crime was committed.

Chapter 18

Standard USI.7b—Identify the basic principles of the new government by the Constitution of the United States of America and the Bill of Rights. Correlates with USI.1a, USI.1b, and USI.1d.

Sharing the Power

After the founding fathers realized the shortcomings in the Articles of Confederation, they met again and this time used what they had learned to create the Constitution of the United States of America. It established a federal system of government. A federal system of government divides the power of government between national government and the governments of the states.

FEDERAL SYSTEM

A failure of the Articles of Confederation was having a Congress which could make laws, but not having any other group to enforce them…or having a group to decide if the laws were fair. The new basic principles of government included separation of powers and a system of checks and balances.

The Constitution called for three separate branches of government. This is called separation of powers. Three separate branches of government also makes sure that no one branch can have more power than the others. Each branch can check the power of the other two. This is called checks and balances. Governmental checks keep any one branch from gaining too much power.

James Madison's "Virginia Plan" was used as the basis for the Constitution of the United States. It called for three separate branches of government:

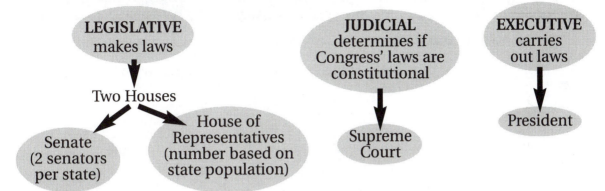

Each branch is dependent on the others to work effectively. Each branch has separate, distinct powers that cannot be taken away by either of the other two branches.

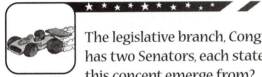

The legislative branch, Congress, is divided into two houses. Since each state has two Senators, each state is represented equally. What earlier document did this concept emerge from? _____

The other house in Congress is the House of Representatives. The number of representatives a state has is based on its population.

What states do you think would have the most representatives? _____

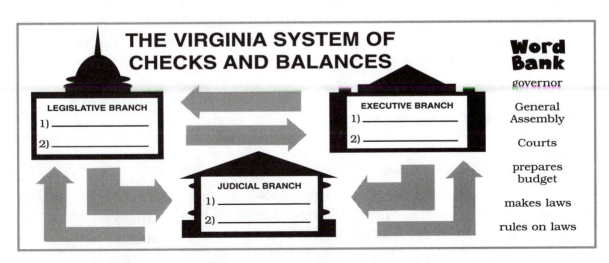

LEGISLATIVE ○ JUDICIAL ○ EXECUTIVE

 How did the new United States government of 1789 differ from that of England?

_____

How many branches of government does the United States have today?

_____

What does this say about James Madison's plan of separation of powers?

_____

_____

Individual Rights Guaranteed

James Madison wrote a document called the Bill of Rights. These are the first 10 amendments to the Constitution of the United States of America. They are a written guarantee of individual rights. Individual rights include the right to freedom of speech, freedom of religion, and freedom to vote.

 guarantee: a promise

 James Madison was the shortest president. He was only 5 feet, 4 inches tall! John Adams' wife, Catherine, described him as "a *very* small man in his *person*, with a *very* large *head*."

Look at a copy of the Bill of Rights to see what rights are guaranteed to all Americans.

Match the rights given to us in the Constitution below with an example.

Example: You are given the right to bear arms. This means you can own a gun.

_____ 1. Freedom of speech   A. you can attend the church of your choice

_____ 2. Freedom of the press   B. you don't have to spend a long time in jail before trial

_____ 3. Right to speedy trial   C. you can go to meetings

_____ 4. Right to vote   D. a newspaper can publish people's opinions

_____ 5. Right to assemble   E. you are allowed to choose your president

_____ 6. Freedom of religion   F. you can criticize your government

_____ 7. Right of trial by jury   G. a group of people will decide what happens to you if you commit a crime

What groups from the colonies' earliest days may have influenced freedom of religion?

_____

_____

_____

Chapter 19

Standard USI.7c—Identify the conflicts that resulted in the emergence of two political parties. Correlates with USI.1b, and USI.1d.

Differences Lead to Splits

The founding fathers had done a good job of getting along and working in agreement when they were creating the government for the new nation. When George Washington was elected president, he hoped no political parties would emerge. He believed everyone should support the Constitution and unite in making new policies.

When Washington named Alexander Hamilton and Thomas Jefferson as his advisors, he put together two men who had very different ideas about government and its purposes. Hamilton was the leader of the Federalist party; he wanted a strong central government. Many people disapproved of Hamilton's programs because they were very similar to those of the British.

Jefferson didn't favor a strong central government. He believed a strong central government didn't consider states' rights. He also thought a strong government would hurt farmers. Jefferson and James Madison began forming a new political party, the Democratic-Republican party.

This table shows the differences between the two parties.

AMERICA'S FIRST POLITICAL PARTIES

FEDERALIST	DEMOCRATIC-REPUBLICAN
Led by Alexander Hamilton	Led by Thomas Jefferson
Favored strong national government	Favored a weak national government
Favored limits on states' powers	Supported states' powers
Favored development of business and industry on a national scale	Favored small business and farmers
Favored a national bank	Opposed a national bank

The debate over the role of national government began in the early days of the nation, and it has continued throughout the history of the United States.

 Read the following statements and determine which of the two early political parties they apply to. Put an F beside those that are Federalist ideas and a D beside those that are Democratic-Republican.

1. ____ As the owner of a business in Philadelphia, I belong to the party that should help my business grow.

2. ____ We have seen what a strong national government does for the people—nothing. The British showed us that. All a strong national government will do is take from the people without giving them anything in return.

3. ____ I live in the state of Virginia. I want my state government to be strong because it is near me and I can tell my representatives my needs.

4. ____ A national bank would be good because it would allow Congress to regulate money and trade and make sure that businesses are treated fairly.

5. ____ A national bank?!?!? I have read the Constitution of the United States several times, and not once does it mention a national bank. If it's not mentioned in the Constitution, we don't need it.

 In the blanks write the name of the person who started the first national political parties.

_____ _____

FEDERALIST   DEMOCRATIC-REPUBLICAN

Chapter 20

Standard USI.7d—Describe the major accomplishments of the first five presidents. Correlates with USI.1a, USI.1c, USI.1d, and USI.1h.

Being the First to Get the Job Done

Congress and the first five presidents made decisions establishing a strong government that helped the nation grow in size and power. The first five presidents faced many challenges in their position, but all were able to make major accomplishments that are still obvious to us today.

During the administration of **George Washington**—

- a federal court system was established
- political parties grew out of disagreements between Thomas Jefferson and Alexander Hamilton over the role of the national government
- the Bill of Rights was added to the U.S. Constitution
- plans were initiated for the national capital to be located in Washington, D.C. An African-American astronomer and surveyor named Benjamin Banneker created the design.

During **John Adams'** administration, a two-party political system emerged.

While **Thomas Jefferson** was president, he bought the territory called Louisiana from France. This big land deal was known as the Louisiana Purchase. Jefferson also appointed Lewis and Clark to explore the land west of the Mississippi River, which was part of the Louisiana Purchase.

James Madison's presidency was during the outbreak of the War of 1812. Madison's strong leadership during this difficult time caused European nations to gain respect for the United States.

While **James Monroe** served as president, he introduced the Monroe Doctrine. It warned European nations not to interfere in the Western Hemisphere.

Amazingly, four of the first five presidents were from Virginia! John Adams was the only one who was not from Virginia.

 Look at the documents listed below and circle those that are primary source documents.

   Monroe Doctrine

   Book about Virginia's presidents

   Bill of Rights

   Benjamin Banneker's plans for the city of Washington, D.C.

   William Clark's journal of the exploration of the Louisiana Purchase

   Thomas Jefferson's sales receipt for the Louisiana Purchase

Look at the following events that took place during the first five presidents' time in office. Put them in the order in which they occurred, starting with the one that happened first. Write the number on the line before the event.

ⓐ ____ The War of 1812 _____

ⓑ ____ The Bill of Rights becomes part of the U.S. Constitution _____

ⓒ ____ The Louisiana Purchase _____

ⓓ ____ The Monroe Doctrine _____

ⓔ ____ Two political parties emerge _____

On the line after each event, write the initials of the man who was president when the event took place.

In the Monroe Doctrine, James Monroe wrote that the Western Hemisphere was in a "free and independent condition," and that the countries in the Western Hemisphere "are henceforth not to be considered as subjects for future colonization by any European powers."

1. By "subjects," what did Monroe mean? _____

2. By "powers," what did he mean? _____

Fitting Together Like a Puzzle

Below are some puzzle pieces. Those on the top represent the first five presidents of the United States. The piece of the puzzle that fits will show an event that took place during the time period each was serving as president. Draw a line from each president piece to the piece which fits his administration.

James Monroe   George Washington   Thomas Jefferson   James Madison   John Adams

Plans for Washington, D.C., were in the works

Appointed Lewis and Clark to explore Louisiana Purchase

Countries in the Western Hemisphere are independent

Europe begins respecting U.S.

A two-party political system emerges

Section VII

History, Geography, and Economics: Expanding Westward!

Chapter 21

Standard USI.8a—Describe territorial expansion and how it affected the United States' political map. Correlates with USI.1c and USI.1f.

Taking on New Territory

Between 1801 and 1861, Americans began to explore the land farther and farther west. This was encouraged, and the United States began to grow as more territories were added. Following the explorations, more people moved to the new land and started settlements.

The main territories added to the United States between 1801 and 1861 were:
- Florida
- the Louisiana Purchase
- Texas
- California
- Oregon

The first land gain for America came during Thomas Jefferson's presidency. In 1803, he bought land from France in a deal that was called the Louisiana Purchase. When this territory was added to the states, the size of the nation doubled!

In 1804, Meriwether Lewis and William Clark, hired by Jefferson, set out on an expedition to explore the land included in the Louisiana Purchase. The expedition started on the Mississippi River where it meets the Missouri River. The explorers followed the Missouri to the Rocky Mountains. They crossed the rugged mountains and kept going until they reached the Pacific Ocean.

1801 —Thomas Jefferson becomes president
_____ —Jefferson makes Louisiana Purchase
1804 —Lewis and Clark expedition
1805 —Lewis and Clark reach Pacific Ocean

Add the missing date to the timeline to show when the Louisiana Purchase was made.

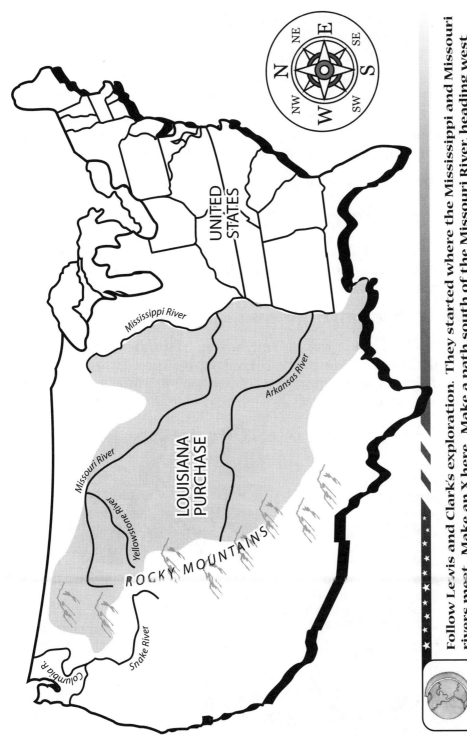

Follow Lewis and Clark's exploration. They started where the Mississippi and Missouri rivers meet. Make an X here. Make a path south of the Missouri River, heading west until the Missouri ends in the Rocky Mountains. Make the route along the river a solid line. Plod through the Rocky Mountains, using a dashed line to show your tracks. Once you're out of the Rocky Mountains, head west to the Pacific Ocean on a trail just above where the Columbia River flows into the ocean.

After a brief rest, load up and head back east. Your route this time is just south of the Columbia River. Cross the Snake River and move southeast until you reach the Yellowstone River. Head north of the Yellowstone until you hit the Missouri River. Put a star here. What a trip!

 Lewis and Clark relied heavily on an important American Indian guide during their journey. The guide was Sacagawea, a teen-age girl who had a baby just before the group set out. She knew routes through terrain. She carried her baby bundled on her back. Lewis and Clark called the baby Pompey. Sacagawea could communicate with other American Indians. She also knew plants that kept the group from starving. Without her help, Lewis and Clark might not have reached the Pacific Ocean.

A Sunny Addition

In 1819, Spain turned over the piece of land called Florida to the United States. This was done through a treaty. In 1821, the United States made Florida into an official U.S. territory.

 In the early 1800s, Florida was the only region in southeastern North America that did not belong to the United States. Throughout its history, the flags of three nations have flown over Florida: Spain, England, and the United States.

The State that Began As a Nation

The state we know as Texas started out as a Spanish possession. In the early 1820s, Americans anxious to farm in new areas convinced the Spanish government to let them settle in the land west of Louisiana and north of the Rio Grande. However, just as people began moving there, Spain lost a war with Mexico, and Mexico took control of Texas.

More and more Americans moved to Texas. They began outnumbering the Mexican citizens, so Mexico began blocking Americans from moving to Texas. Tensions rose between the two groups because the Americans, who were also called Anglos, began disobeying the Mexican laws. Mexico saw this as the Anglos' way of starting a revolt. Soon, a full-blown war broke out.

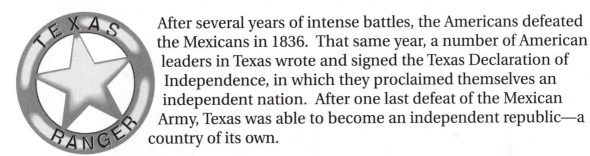

After several years of intense battles, the Americans defeated the Mexicans in 1836. That same year, a number of American leaders in Texas wrote and signed the Texas Declaration of Independence, in which they proclaimed themselves an independent nation. After one last defeat of the Mexican Army, Texas was able to become an independent republic—a country of its own.

The leaders who made sure that Texas became an independent republic wanted it to become a state, but that was hard because Mexico had said it would declare war against the United States if Texas was granted statehood. Northerners also didn't want to admit Texas to the Union because it would be a slave state and most northern states opposed slavery. The Texas leaders were tricky, though, and told the U.S. leaders that if the United States wouldn't welcome Texas into the Union, maybe France or England would. At the threat, Congress moved quickly, and Texas became a state on December 29, 1845.

Unlike the other states, Texas became part of the United States as a full-fledged state—not as a territory. Texas was the only state to enter the United States after being a nation all by itself.

Put the following nations in order of when they claimed Texas. Label them 1, 2, and 3.

A. _____ Mexico   B. _____ Spain   C. _____ United States

Oh, It's Another New Territory—Oregon!

Following the expedition of Lewis and Clark and reports of plentiful beaver, many trappers flocked to the extreme western lands. These were rugged frontiersmen from the colonies, as well as Europeans and Canadians.

When the War of 1812 broke out, the British captured an American outpost on the Columbia River and controlled it for many years. Finally, the British moved on and started a new fort farther up the Columbia River. They built a large settlement and firmly established themselves.

More and more people from the East began moving west—trappers, missionaries, and farmers. Before long, a well-marked trail showed the way. The United States felt it had claim to the area, and so did England. The dispute was settled in 1846 when the British decided to give up their claim to the land below the 49th parallel of latitude. There were just too many Americans for the British to deal with!

In the 1840s, pioneers began making their way westward to settle Oregon Territory. They took a route called the Oregon Trail. Ruts left by the wheels of their wagons can still be seen today along some sections of the Oregon Trail.

This map shows the border between Canada and the United States that was decided in 1846. What is the parallel of latitude where this border lies? _____th

California, Here We Come!

When Texas joined the Union, Mexico threatened to wage war against the United States. They kept their promise. The United States claimed that the Rio Grande was the southern border of the United States, but Mexico disagreed. American soldiers went to the area to protect the U.S. claim, and Mexican soldiers attacked them. In 1846, the United States declared war on Mexico.

In 1848, Mexico surrendered and a treaty ended the war. The treaty also gave the United States nearly 2 million acres of land, which included land that would become the state of California and other southwestern states.

Now the territories of the United States stretched from the Atlantic Ocean to the Pacific Ocean—from sea to shining sea.

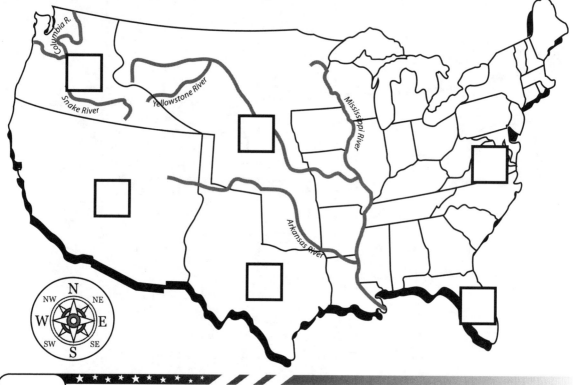

 Look at this map and number the region in the order in which the land was added to the possessions of the United States.

Chapter 22

Standard USI.8b—Identify geographic and economic factors that influenced the westward movement of settlers. Correlates with USI.1b, USI.1d, and USI.1f.

New Places to Go, New Ways to Get There

The promise of unsettled land and the opportunity to make money influenced many pioneers to move westward. Many Americans believed that since the United States had abundant land they could continue moving westward. They believed that this expansion was good for the country and was their right. This belief is called the right of "Manifest Destiny."

What reasons would have caused so many pioneers to pack up and move west?

- The population of the East had grown. The East was becoming too crowded. People wanted more space between themselves and their neighbors.

- Land in the West was basically there for the taking. There was lots of it, and it was cheap. It held the promise of fertile fields.

- The West offered economic opportunity. The California Gold Rush drew many people over the Rocky Mountains. Logging and farming were also rumored to be good money-making jobs. Slaves who managed to escape could also see promise in the West—the promise of freedom.

- Transportation improvements also made it cheaper and faster to go west. Canals, such as the Erie Canal, were constructed to make transportation routes shorter. The invention of the steamboat also made the trip West easier.

- People were learning of overland trails, such as the Oregon and Sante Fe trails.

These factors all supported the practice of Manifest Destiny.

Match the mode of transportation people moving west would have taken with the route they used.

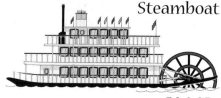
Steamboat

Oregon Trail

Covered wagon

Erie Canal

Today, when people want to travel from the east to the west, what are the main modes of transportation they use?

_____ and _____

 Below are several people. Determine what they hope to find by moving westward.

"I am going west to start a new life. I hope I will find a job there, but after being a slave, the best thing I will find is _____."

"I have heard that there are many tremendous trees in the Oregon Territory. I am planning to start a career in _____."

"We get reports that they're finding nuggets the size of marbles in California…nuggets of _____, that is."

"I want to start a big farm, maybe grow some corn or wheat. I have been told there's lots of fertile _____ in the west, and it's cheap and plentiful!"

Look at this map of the United States. Draw a line from each item or person to the region where it was usually found.

In 1846, a group of 87 people led by a man named George Donner decided to go west. They started on the Oregon Trail, planning to reach the California Trail. Someone suggested a shortcut. Soon, they knew that was a bad choice. The new trail was too narrow. Winter set in and the group was stranded in the Sierra Mountains. There was no game to hunt. Before long, the oxen and mules pulling the wagons died. The people had to eat them! Finally, help came at the end of the winter. Only 41 people had survived. The path where they had spent the horrible winter is still called Donner's Pass.

Chapter 23

Standard USI.8c—Describe the impact of inventions on westward expansion in the United States from 1801 to 1861. Correlates with USI.1b and USI.1c.

The Impact of Inventions

Before the Civil War, most industrialization in America was in the North. Agriculture was more common in the South. Even though equipment was produced and used more in the North, it still had an effect on the farming society of the South.

For example, Eli Whitney invented the cotton gin. Whitney was from the North originally, but while he was working as a tutor in Georgia, he developed a simple machine that would separate seeds from the fibers of cotton. The machine was inexpensive and easy to make. It increased the production of cotton. As a result of increasing the production of cotton, Southern plantations needed more slaves to cultivate and pick the cotton.

cultivate: to plant and grow, especially crops

Another important invention was the reaper. Cyrus McCormick and a slave named Jo Anderson invented the reaper. Reapers were used to harvest grain. They separated the grain from the plant stems. The reaper increased the amount of work American farmers could do.

Jo Anderson was a slave on Cyrus McCormick's farm. He worked beside McCormick at all stages of building and testing the reaper. Some said the two were more like brothers than slave and master.

Look at these pictures and number them in order.

Steaming Ahead!

Robert Fulton improved the steamboat. This was a very important invention because it eventually provided faster river transportation. The steamboat strengthened the connection between the Western territories the Northern industries and the plantations and farms of the South.

While the steamboat made transportation by water much quicker, the steam locomotive provided faster land transportation.

Look at these modes of transportation. Put them in order of the earliest to the latest.

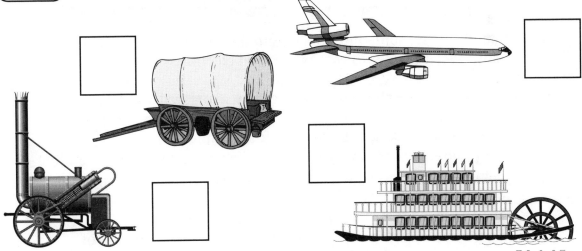

Which mode of transportation do we use most often today? _____

Match the inventor with his invention.

1. Cyrus McCormick   2. Robert Fulton   3. Eli Whitney

A. steamboat   B. cotton gin   C. reaper

Chapter 24

Standard USI.8d—Identify the main ideas of the abolitionist and suffrage movements. Correlates with USI.1b, USI.1c, USI.1d, and USI.1h.

All PEOPLE Are Created Equal

Before the Civil War, two issues of all people being treated equally concerned many Americans. The issue of slavery caused many people to become involved in the abolitionist movement, and the issue of women not being able to vote caused many people to become involved in the suffrage movement.

abolitionist: someone who, before the Civil War, fought to end slavery
suffrage: the right to vote in political elections

People involved in the abolitionist movement expressed several key ideas:

- Most demanded that all slaves be freed immediately.
- They believed that slavery was wrong for several reasons, including being morally wrong, which means it was not a good or right thing in people's lives.
- They believed that slavery was cruel and inhumane.
- They believed that slavery was a violation of the principles of democracy—that all people are created equal.

The abolitionist movement had both men and women leaders. Well-known abolitionists were:

- Harriet Tubman
- William Lloyd Garrison
- Frederick Douglass

The Same Rights for Women

Supporters of the suffrage movement declared that "All men and women are created equal." They believed that women deserved the same rights as men. Supporters of the suffragist movement believed that women were deprived of basic rights such as:

- the right to vote
- the right to educational opportunities, especially being allowed to attend college
- the right to equal opportunities in business
- the right to own property independently

The suffragist movement was led by several strong women. Their efforts to get equality for women began before the Civil War and continued until after it had ended. Several important leaders in the suffragist movement were:

- Isabel Sojourner Truth
- Susan B. Anthony
- Elizabeth Cady Stanton

 Circle the movement that started before the Civil War and was still going strong after the Civil War ended.

ABOLITIONIST   SUFFRAGIST

The Declaration of Independence contains the phrase "…all men are created equal." The suffragists added an important word to this phrase. What is it?

_____

Leaders of the abolitionist and suffragist movements spoke out about people being treated unfairly. Today, people sometimes show their dissatisfaction with what is going on. Sometimes they give speeches or participate in protests. Look at the words below and circle the ones that might cause people to protest today.

PAY CUTS	FLAT TIRES	SPEED LIMITS
SPRAINED ANKLES	MOVIE TICKET PRICES	A WAR

Look at the statements below and decide if they belong to an abolitionist or a suffragist. Circle A if the quote is from an abolitionist, or S if it's from a suffragist.

1. **A S** Women should be allowed to go to college.

2. **A S** I try to go to all of the speeches given by Susan B. Anthony.

3. **A S** I believe that all slaves should be freed…NOW!

4. **A S** Slavery is a violation of the principles of democracy.

5. **A S** Women should have the right to own property.

6. **A S** Voting is a right women should have.

Look at the names listed here. Beside each name, write A f the person was known for being an abolitionist, or S if a suffragist.

___ Susan B. Anthony   ___ Elizabeth Cady Stanton

___ Frederick Douglass   ___ Isabel Sojourner Truth

___ William Lloyd Garrison   ___ Harriet Tubman

Harriet Tubman became a famous "conductor" on the Underground Railroad, a system of moving escaped slaves from the South to the North where they could be considered free. She was never caught and she never lost a "passenger." There was even a $40,000 reward for her capture—dead or alive!

Section VIII

History, Geography, and Economics:

The Civil War: Causes, Events, and Effects

Chapter 25

Standard USI.9a—Describe the cultural, economic, and constitutional issues that divided the nation leading up to the Civil War. Correlates with USI.1b, USI.1c, and USI.1d.

Heading for Division

As the United States grew older, clear differences showed up between the North and the South. The differences were cultural, which dealt with how people of the two regions lived their lives. The differences were economic, which dealt with how the people of the two regions made their livings and earned money. Finally, the differences were constitutional, which dealt with how the people of both regions viewed the U.S. Constitution.

While there were several differences between the North and the South, the issues related to slavery kept growing larger and leading to major disagreements that divided the nation and led to the Civil War.

Imagine you're from the North. What are your feelings about slavery?

_____

_____

_____

On the issue of slavery, would the average person from the South share the feelings of the average person from the North? How would their opinions be different?

_____

_____

Cultural Matters

Because of their cultural differences, people of the North and South had difficulties agreeing on social and political issues. In the North, people lived mainly in an urban society, or in towns and cities. People in the North held jobs. The South was more rural. It was mainly an agricultural society. People lived in small villages and on farms and plantations.

 Which of these homes would have been found in the North and which would have been in the South? Write your answer on the line beneath the picture.

_____   _____

A Matter of Economics

The North was a manufacturing region. The people there made goods and products. Northerners favored tariffs that protected factory owners and workers from foreign competition. Goods and products from foreign countries were taxed before they could enter the United States. This allowed the Northern manufacturers to sell goods less expensively and discouraged foreign countries from importing their goods. They probably could not make enough money to make selling things in the United States profitable.

 tariff: a list of taxes on goods that are brought into the country to be sold; goods made to be sold outside the country can also be tariffed

Southerners protested high tariffs because they increased the costs of products from other countries that the farmers needed. Cotton planters in the South also worried that England would stop buying cotton if they had to pay too many high tariffs.

 Look at these statements. On the space before each, write N if it was said by a Northerner or S if it was said by a Southerner.

NORTHERNER   SOUTHERNER

_____ I live in a large city with lots of other people.

_____ I am an overseer on a plantation that grows cotton.

_____ I am strongly opposed to slavery.

_____ I do not have a problem with plantations using slaves.

_____ I work in a factory that makes ship anchors.

_____ I believe tariffs are good.

_____ Tariffs could put me out of business.

The Issue of Constitutionality

The final issue that led to the start of the Civil War was the difference between how Northerners and Southerners felt about the U.S. Constitution and the power it gave government. Northerners supported a strong central government, while Southerners thought states should have more power than the national government.

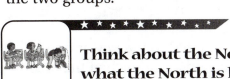

The line between the North and South was became even clearer. Anger steadily built between the two groups.

Think about the North before the Civil War and then about what the North is like today. Look at the following list and cross off the item(s) that are not an issue in the North today.

The region was industrial.   People lived in cities.   Most Northerners opposed slavery.

Think about the South as it was before the Civil War and then about what you think the South is like today. Cross the item(s) from the list that no longer apply to the South today.

Plantations were common in the South.   Southerners strongly supported states' rights.

Agriculture was the only economic activity in the South.

Look at each date and write the letter that corresponds to it in the box.

A. Civil War begins

B. Colonies united as nation.

C. Differences begin separating North and South

1780   1850   1861

Chapter 26

Standard USI.9b—Explain how the issues of states' rights and slavery increased sectional tensions. Correlates with USI.1c, USI.1d, and USI.1h.

A House Divided

The issue of states' rights and slavery drove a wedge between the North and South. As time passed, tension between the two sections of the nation became greater and greater.

One important issue that separated the country related to the power of the Federal government. On one side, Southerners believed that they had the power to decide if any national law was illegal. If they believed a law was illegal, they didn't have to obey it. On the opposite side, Northerners believed that national laws were the strongest laws—the national government's power was higher than that of the states'.

The South was afraid that the North would take control of Congress and begin doing away with states' rights. As a result, Southerners began to proclaim states' rights as a mean of self-protection. The North believed that the nation was a union, a group of states joined as one that could not be divided.

Abraham Lincoln campaigned to become a senator in Illinois in 1858. He opened his campaign with a speech that included this famous line: "A house divided against itself cannot stand."

1. What was Lincoln referring to with the word "house"? _____

2. What was Lincoln saying would happen to the "house" if it divided? _____
_____

3. What issues were dividing the "house" in 1858? _____

Economics Versus Morals

Slavery was another issue that caused the two sections of the United States to differ. While the Civil War did not begin as a war to abolish slavery, the issue did divide the country. Southerners felt that the abolition of slavery would destroy their region's economy. Northerners believed that slavery was very wrong and should be abolished for moral reasons.

A Stitch in Time Saves Nine

Benjamin Franklin wrote, "A stitch in time saves nine." What he meant was that if a repair is made when a tear is first noticed, it is not nearly as hard to fix than if the tear is left alone and allowed to become worse. The government leaders of the mid-1800s could see that the nation was starting to tear. They started trying to make repairs before the tear became worse.

One measure the federal government took to resolve differences between the North and South was to create compromises that balanced the number of states that had slaves with the number of those that didn't.

compromise: settlement of an argument by each side giving up something

The first compromise was made in 1820 with the Missouri Compromise. Missouri applied for statehood. Some people in Missouri owned slaves. At the time there were 22 states in the nation—11 were slave states and 11 were free states. Statehood for Missouri would have meant that there were more slave states than free states. When Maine applied for statehood as a free state, the number was balanced again. Both Maine and Missouri became states in 1820.

Lawmakers also decided to decrease the areas that might apply for statehood as slave states. Slavery would not be allowed north of the 36°30' north latitude.

Another compromise was reached in 1850. With the Compromise of 1850, California entered the nation as a free state. The southwest territories could decide for themselves if they wanted to be slave or free states.

The Kansas-Nebraska Act was passed in 1854. It allowed the people living in the territories to decide if they wanted to allow slavery in their areas. Allowing people to decide issues such as these was called "popular sovereignty." In terms of popular sovereignty, the side that had the most votes won!

sovereignty: the condition of having independent political power

Put these legislative events in the order in which they took place.

1. ____ Compromise of 1850

2. ____ Kansas-Nebraska Act

3. ____ Missouri Compromise

A Succession of Secessions

Abraham Lincoln made no effort to hide the fact that he opposed slavery. When his friends encouraged him to run for the presidency in 1860, he gave speeches saying that slavery should be kept only in the states where it had been going on. Slavery should not be allowed to take place in new territories, he said. His goal was to keep the nation together because the South was leaning more and more toward separating from the rest of the nation. Lincoln and many Northerners believed that the United States was one nation that could not be separated or divided. Many Southerners, however, believed that states had freely created and joined the union, and if they decided to leave it, they could freely do that too.

When Lincoln was elected late in 1860, many Southern states seceded from the Union. Southern tempers flared, and Confederate forces attacked Fort Sumter in South Carolina. The Civil War had begun!

secede: to stop being a member of a group

Southerners began firing on Fort Sumter on April 12, 1861. After hundreds of shells struck the fort and fire threatened to cause an explosion, Major Robert Anderson surrendered. On April 14, he ordered a 50-gun salute to the U.S. flag. The only person to die at Fort Sumter was killed when the last gun exploded during the salute.

Fill in the blanks with the correct answer.

People in the North and the South saw things very differently in the late mid-1800s. They viewed the _____ of the Federal government differently. Those in the South believed they had the power to declare national laws _____ if they did not want to obey them, while people in the North believed that the national government's power was _____ over that of the states.

Slavery was an important issue leading up to the Civil War. It deeply divided the nation on a line between the North and South. Southerners believed that abolishing slavery would destroy the South's _____. Northerners believed that slavery should be abolished for _____ reasons.

Many people in the North believed that the Union was one nation and could not be _____, while Southerners saw the Union as something they had freely joined and something that they could freely _____.

WORD BANK

| authority | divided | economy | illegal |
| leave | moral | supreme | |

Chapter 27

Standard USI.9c—Identify on a map the states that seceded from the Union and those that remained in the Union. Correlates with USI.1f.

Coming Apart at the Seams

The states that seceded from the United States during the Civil War were those that depended on agriculture to earn a living. Agricultural states depended on labor-intensive cash crops. "Labor-intensive" is another way of saying that a lot of work from people is required. The states that depended on agriculture generally depended on slaves to do the work. Some slave states chose not to leave the Union. These states were the northernmost slave states of Delaware, Kentucky, Maryland, and Missouri.

The states that seceded from the nation were:

Alabama	Georgia	Mississippi	Tennessee
Arkansas	Louisiana	North Carolina	Louisiana
Texas	Florida	South Carolina	Virginia

The states that remained in the Union were:

California	Maine	New York	West Virginia
Connecticut	Massachusetts	Ohio	(the western counties of
Illinois	Michigan	Oregon	Virginia that refused to
Indiana	Minnesota	Pennsylvania	secede from the Union)
Iowa	New Hampshire	Rhode Island	Wisconsin
Kansas	New Jersey	Vermont	

This map shows how the United States looked in 1861. Some of the states are numbered. On each numbered line, write the name of the state it matches. Then write an S if it was a slave state, an F if it was a free state, or a B if it was a border state that continued to have slaves but remained a member of the Union during the Civil War.

1) _____ ____
2) _____ ____
3) _____ ____
4) _____ ____
5) _____ ____
6) _____ ____
7) _____ ____
8) _____ ____

9) _____ ____
10) _____ ____
11) _____ ____
12) _____ ____
13) _____ ____
14) _____ ____
15) _____ ____

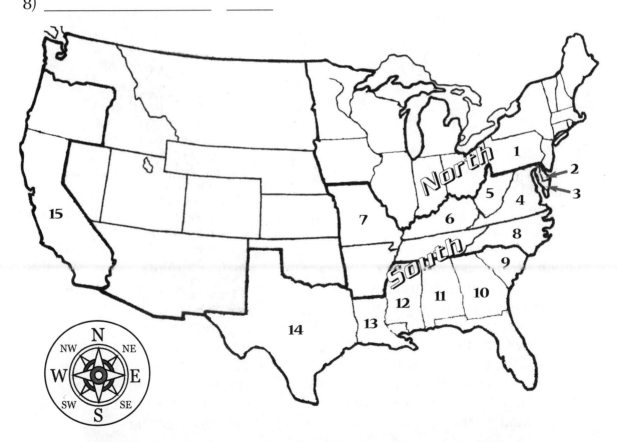

Chapter 28

Standard USI.9d—Describe the roles of Abraham Lincoln, Jefferson Davis, Ulysses S. Grant, Robert E. Lee, Thomas "Stonewall" Jackson, and Frederick Douglass in events leading to and during the war. Correlates with USI.1a, USI.1c, and USI.1d.

When Two Great Minds Collide

Abraham Lincoln and Robert E. Lee were two men who were very powerful in the time leading up to and during the Civil War. These two men represented very different views of the nature of the United States. With their positions as leaders and their differences in opinion, conflict was bound to happen.

As a Civil War leader, Abraham Lincoln:

- was President of the United States, elected in 1860
- opposed the spread of slavery
- issued the Emancipation Proclamation
- was determined to preserve the Union—by force, if necessary
- believed the United States was one nation, not a collection of independent states
- wrote the Gettysburg Address that said the Civil War, which began in 1861, was to preserve a government "of the people, by the people, and for the people"

As a Civil War leader, Robert E. Lee:

- was the leader of the Army of Northern Virginia
- was offered the command of the Union forces at the beginning of the war, but chose not to fight against Virginia
- opposed secession, but did not believe the union should be held together by force
- urged Southerners to accept defeat at the end of the war and reunite as Americans when some wanted to continue fighting

Robert E. Lee was an officer in the United States Army before the Civil War began. He was offered the command of the Union Army to help end the rebellion in the South. However, the state of Virginia seceded, so Lee felt it was his duty to defend his native Virginia, which he considered was being invaded by a hostile force.

TRUE OR FALSE? If Virginia had remained a member of the Union, Robert E. Lee would still have commanded the Confederate Army. _____

Make a timeline of some of the key events in Lincoln's career as a leader using the dates shown here. Put them in the order in which they occurred on the timeline, from the first to last. Two are left for you to add.

1862 — Emancipation Proclamation

1863 — Gettysburg Address

1861 — _____

_____ — Elected president

1. Look at the items from Abraham Lincoln's timeline. Which two are primary source documents?

_____ and _____

2. In the Gettysburg Address, Lincoln mentions preserving a government "of the people, by the people, and for the people." What other important American historical document mentions this?

_____
_____

The Gettysburg Address begins, "Four score and seven years ago…" A "score" is 20 years. How long ago was "four score and seven years"?

 _____ years

Other Civil War Leaders

 Ulysses S. Grant was general of the Union army that defeated Robert E. Lee and the Confederate Army.

Jefferson Davis was president of the Confederate States of America.

Frederick Douglass was a former slave who escaped to the North and became an abolitionist.

Thomas "Stonewall" Jackson was a skilled Confederate general from Virginia. He earned the nickname "Stonewall" during the First Battle of Manassas (Bull Run). A general saw him bravely facing the enemy and said, "There is Jackson, standing like a stone wall."

 Read the quotes and decide who may have said them. Write the person's name on the line beneath the quote.

1. As a former slave, I know how unfairly slaves are treated. It is not right for one man to think he can own another.

   _____

2. The rights of states are very important. If the Union is allowed to control us, we will lose our independence. As president of the Confederacy, it is up to me to make sure that states' rights are preserved.

   _____

3. My army is bound to win this war. We have more railroads and a larger government to back us. The factories and the railroads in the North are also a help to us.

   _____

Chapter 29

Standard USI.9e—Use maps to explain critical developments in the war, including maj[or battles]. Correlates with USI.1a, USI.1c, USI.1f, and USI.1h.

On the Offensive and the Defensive

Important developments in the Civil War, especially major battles, took place in both the North and South. Locations and topography were critical elements that played a part in where the developments took place. Each army was trying to hold on to its important cities and transportation routes such as ports and rivers…while trying to take the other side's important cities and transportation routes.

> More Americans died during the Civil War than World Wars I and II combined, and Virginia was the site of more Civil War battles than any other state!

A few major battles and events during the Civil War include these events:

- April 12, 1861—Confederate forces fire on Fort Sumter, South Carolina, beginning the war.

- July 21, 1861—The First Battle of Manassas (Bull Run) becomes the first battle of the Civil War.

- September 22, 1862—President Lincoln signs the Emancipation Proclamation, freeing slaves in slave states that did not return to the Union by January 1, 1863.

- March–July, 1863—At the Battle of Vicksburg, a defeat of Southern troops divides the South, with the North taking control of the Mississippi River.

- July 1863—The Battle of Gettysburg becomes the turning point in the war, with the North repelling Robert E. Lee's invasion.

- April 9, 1865—General Robert E. Lee surrenders for the Confederacy at Appomattox Court House, Virginia.

He Who Has the Capital Wins!

Battle locations often were decided as each army attempted to capture the capital of the other side. The enemy's capital city was a prize each side was trying to win. Capturing a capital was a sure victory and an end to the war.

Why do you think so many battles took place in Virginia?

_____

_____

Richmond was the capital of the Confederacy during the last part of the Civil War. Put a star on this city. The capital of the Union was Washington, D.C. Put a √ on this city. The terms of the surrender of the South were detailed at Appomattox Court House. Put an S on this city.

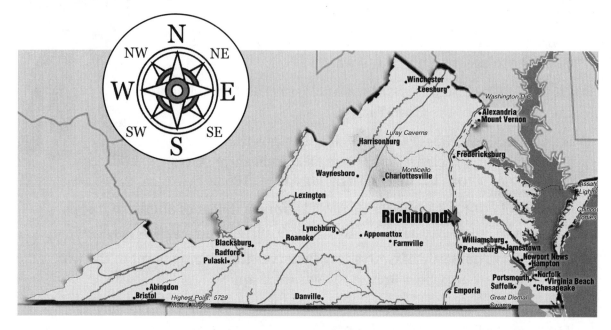

©2004 Carole Marsh/Gallopade International • 800-536-2GET • www.virginiaexperience.com • Page 128

~ This book is not reproducible. ~

Here is a map of the eastern United States as it looked during the Civil War. Some critical areas from the Civil War are shown. Beside each is a box. Number them in the order that events took place.

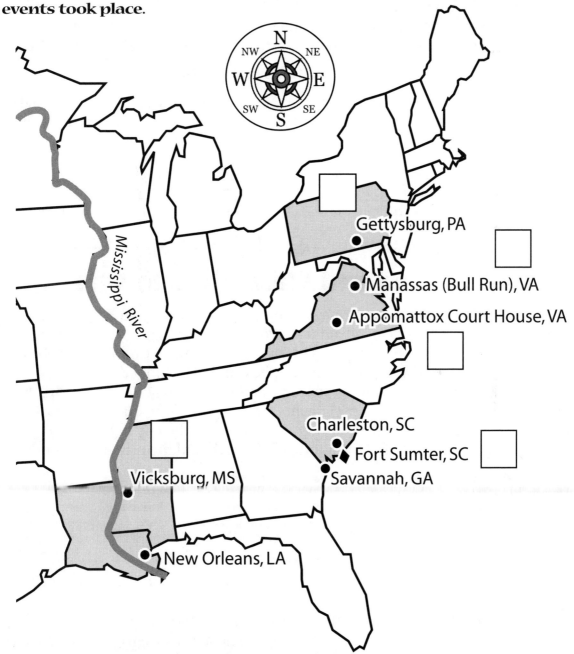

Freedom Proclaimed

Abraham Lincoln issued the Emancipation Proclamation on September 22, 1862. It said that slaves of the states that had seceded would be freed if those states did not return to the Union by January 1, 1863. "Freeing the slaves" became a new focus of the war. Many former slaves joined the Union army and aided the North in its effort.

In the Emancipation Proclamation, Lincoln wrote: "And I further declare and make known that such persons of suitable condition will be received into the armed service of the United States…" What did he mean by this?

The Emancipation Proclamation ____ IS ____ IS NOT a primary source document.

What Land and Water Have to Offer

During the Civil War, the main strategy of the commanders was to keep or take areas that would give them an advantage. Port cities were important. As long as the South had control of the key ports of Savannah, Georgia; Charleston, South Carolina; and New Orleans, Louisiana, supplies could be shipped in from the European countries. Union troops seized Charleston in May 1861. On April 29, 1862, they took possession of New Orleans. On December 21, 1864, Union General William T. Sherman occupied Savannah. He presented the city to Lincoln as a Christmas gift. Without ports, the South was cut off from the rest of the world!

1. Which was the first Southern port taken by the Union army?
   A. Charleston B. New Orleans C. Savannah

2. Which port city did Sherman give Lincoln for Christmas?
   A. Charleston B. New Orleans C. Savannah

3. Why were port cities important to the South during the Civil War?
A. for boat races B. for seafood C. for receiving supplies from European countries

The Mighty Mississippi

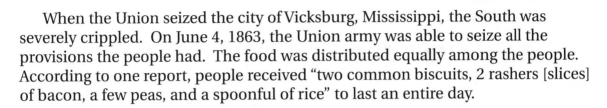

Having control of the Mississippi River was important to both sides. As long as the South had it, provisions and supplies could be boated around in the South. Troops could also move to other locations by boat.

When the Union seized the city of Vicksburg, Mississippi, the South was severely crippled. On June 4, 1863, the Union army was able to seize all the provisions the people had. The food was distributed equally among the people. According to one report, people received "two common biscuits, 2 rashers [slices] of bacon, a few peas, and a spoonful of rice" to last an entire day.

In spite of the attack on Vicksburg, church services took place. Emma Balfour, a member of Christ Episcopal Church, wrote, "With the deep boom of cannon taking the place of organ notes…Reverend W.W. Lord preached the Gospel of eternal peace to an assemblage of powder-grimed and often blood-stained soldiery at Christ's Church."

The siege of Vicksburg lasted 47 days. During that time, people sought shelter and protection by moving into caves. In some cases, as many as 200 people lived in a single cave!

1. The passage above lists the food rations for a day in Vicksburg after the city was seized by the Union Army. Do you think this amount of food left people hungry or satisfied?

_____

2. In her description of a church service during the siege of Vicksburg, Emma Balfour mentions the boom of cannons replacing the sound of what?

_____

3. Emma Balfour mentions "an assemblage." This is

_____ a. one person   _____ b. a group of people

On Higher Ground

Topography decided some battle locations. Higher ground was more desirable because once troops were in position on higher ground they had a better chance of seeing who was coming. The Battle of Gettysburg was the turning point in the war, and the Northern victory left the South with no chance of winning the Civil War.

Here are a few areas that were important during the Civil War. Put a C beside those that were under the control of the Confederacy and a U beside those that were under the control of the Union when the war ended in 1865.

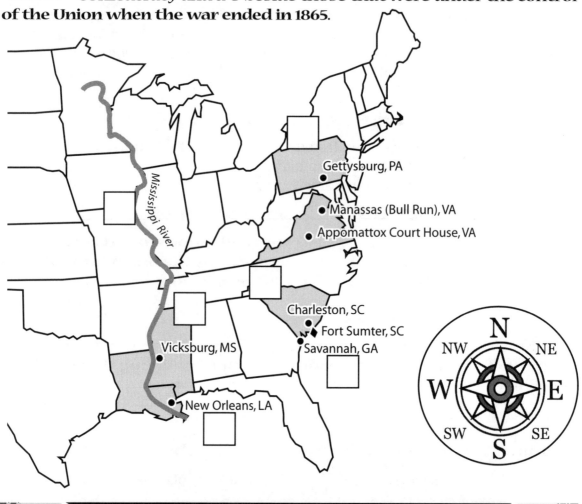

Chapter 30

Standard USI.9f—Describe the effects of war from the perspectives of Union and Confederate soldiers (including black soldiers), women, and slaves.

Battlefield Barriers and Homefront Hardships

During the Civil War, most people faced hardships. Not only did soldiers face challenges, but women and slaves did, too. For many, the hardships were too great to overcome. While soldiers faced cannonballs and bullets on the battlefield, other people of the time fought starvation, diseases, and exposure to the elements of the weather. It was a harsh time in America's history.

One of the saddest effects of the Civil War was families' and friends' opposing each other on the battlefield. When the lines of battle were drawn, former countrymen were put on opposite sides of the conflict. In some cases, men didn't join the army of their home state. They often joined the other side's army.

As the war wore on, many soldiers were killed or injured on both sides, but the Southern forces were especially hard hit. The number of young men old enough to serve in the Army began to decrease, so the average age of Southern troops became younger. Supplies and equipment also became scarce. Before the end of the war, boys were fighting for the South without adequate weapons or clothing.

This is what a new recruit in the Confederate army might have thought.

"This fight won't last long. As a matter of fact, it probably will be over today. I am not sure what we're fighting about, but this will be fun. I'm a little confused because I see some of my cousins from up north on the other side. Oh, my family will be so proud of me. I get to wear a uniform and shoot a rifle. Wow! Look at all the people with their picnic baskets that came out to watch. And look at that pretty girl over there. I think I'll wave at her. Hey! She waved back! I can't wait to get started. I'm sure to impress her. Maybe she will invite me over afterwards!"

Read each statement below. Circle U if a soldier from the Union said it, or C if it from a Confederate soldier.

C U **1.** I am from Virginia. My family was always poor, and we didn't have much land and didn't need slaves. I just can't fight for an army that would want to see people owning other people.

C U **2.** When my father helped found this nation, he did it with the idea that his state would be free to make its own laws and form its own government, not have someone up in Washington, D.C., telling him what to do! I joined the army that supports state's rights.

C U **3.** I am constantly amazed at how General Ulysses Grant leads us. He always makes sure we have the weapons we need to fight, and he makes sure we get plenty to eat.

C U **4.** All the states form a nation, a united nation. No state should be allowed to say they're not going to be part of the Union!

C U **5.** I am only 12. My brother went off to fight and he lost a leg at the Battle of Gettysburg, but he said that General Lee rode by him and told him he was a fine soldier. Since he can't fight now, I am going in his place.

Battles in the Backyard

Since the battlefields of the Civil War were in the states, battles were going on in people's backyards, especially in the South. Homes were destroyed or taken over for military purposes. In many cases, all the able-bodied men had gone to

fight the war, leaving young boys, old men, and women behind to keep everything operating. In the North, women found themselves running businesses. In the South, they managed large plantations.

Determine where each of the speakers in the following sentences were from. Write North or South.

1. I was very scared when Jasper left me to go to the war. I had always managed things in the house, but never the whole plantation before! There was a lot to do. I had to order seed and make sure fields were plowed and everything was planted at the right time. It was hard, but that is what I had to do as a woman in the _____.

2. Fortunately, I had watched Robert work on the books. I was always good in arithmetic. When people brought in payments for our carriages, I marked down what they paid. Then I subtracted it and made them a new bill. I will be glad when Robert returns, though, for handling his business while he away fighting for the _____ has been challenging!

 Look at this bill that Robert's wife prepared. Is it correct. If not, what is the correct balance?

_____

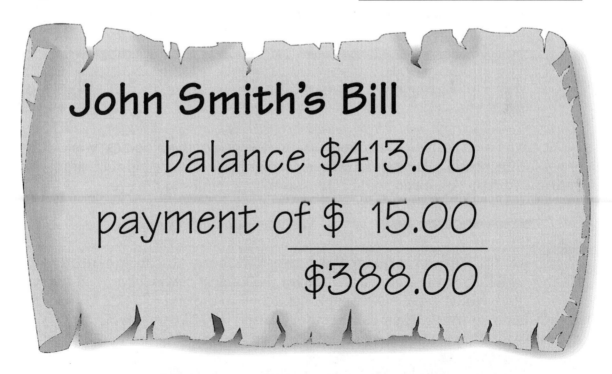

John Smith's Bill

balance $413.00

payment of $ 15.00
_____

$388.00

On Both Sides of the Lines

African Americans were deeply affected by the Civil War. For many, the war was their way to freedom. African Americans fought in both the Confederate and Union armies. In the Union army, they were treated more like real soldiers. The Union enlisted African American sailors early in the war. The Confederacy often used slaves as naval crew members and soldiers.

The focus of the Civil War shifted after Lincoln signed the Emancipation Proclamation. After that, "freeing the slaves" became a goal for the Union army. Even though former slaves were serving in the Union army, they were not given equal treatment.

African American soldiers in the Union army were:
- paid less than white soldiers
- discriminated against
- made to serve in segregated units
- commanded by white officers

Even when they were fighting with people who were saying they would make them equals, the African-American soldiers were not treated equally.

segregated: set apart from others; isolated

The Civil War has always been remembered as one of the bloodiest wars. It is known for the brutal battles and the man-to-man, face-to-face fighting. Both white and African-American soldiers looked their enemies in the eyes.

In the Battle of Millikin's Bend, near Vicksburg, African-American soldiers in the Union army fought the longest bayonet battle of the war. (A bayonet is knifelike weapon attached to the end of a rifle for use in hand-to-hand combat). Their commander praised the soldiers, saying, "It is impossible for men to show greater bravery than the Negro troops in that fight."

Picking Up the Pieces

By the end of the war, much of the South was devastated. Many cities, such as Vicksburg and Richmond, had been shelled until they were in ruins, and the city of Atlanta, Georgia, was a charred mess because General William Sherman and his Northern troops burned the town. Much of the South faced rebuilding.

If the many thousands of deaths from the battles themselves were not bad enough, diseases also became a deadly problem. For every soldier who died of a battle wound, four died from diseases. Many soldiers came from isolated rural areas where they had not been exposed to many diseases and allowed to build up immunities. In the crowded camps of the Army, germs spread like wildfire. Mumps, measles, and smallpox struck thousands. In the South, Northern soldiers died of malaria or yellow fever.

Poor sanitation, lack of proper nutrition, and inadequate medical supplies and equipment killed more—both civilians and military figures—than the war itself.

Angel of the Battlefield

During the Civil War, one woman in particular became well known for her efforts to help others. She was Clara Barton. She collected supplies and took them to the battlefields. She also nursed injured soldiers. She was nicknamed "the angel of the battlefield."

Clara Barton went on to set up the American Red Cross in 1881. She and co-workers brought food and supplies to areas where disasters took place. She directed the American Red Cross until 1904. Today, this organization still takes care of those who need help the most.

Put these important events in Clara Barton's life in order by writing 1, 2, or 3 in the boxes.

☐ Founded American Red Cross

☐ Nurse during Civil War

☐ Stopped being American Red Cross director

Setting His Own Course

During the Civil War, one African American who made a difference was Robert Smalls. Smalls was born a slave in the coastal town of Beaufort, South Carolina. He became an expert boat pilot while sailing in Charleston Harbor.

When the Civil War broke out, Smalls had a daring chance to escape to freedom. In 1861, the Confederate army made Smalls pilot a boat named the *Planter*. It was a messenger and transport steamer. In 1862, he bravely guided the ship out of Charleston Harbor and delivered it to officials in the Union army! They made him a pilot of the *Planter*. Smalls became known for his feats of bravery, and he after the war was over, he was honored for his heroism.

Robert Smalls went on to become a congressman. He served in the South Carolina state legislature and then as a member of the U.S. House of Representatives. His accomplishments were impressive for anyone, but even greater for an African American.

Robert Smalls is piloting the *Planter* on a daring mission in Charleston Harbor. Help him find his way safely to the Union dock.

Show Me the Money!

When the Southern states seceded, they decided they would not use the same money that the Northern states used, so they designed their own currency. They didn't have coins, so they printed paper money called "fractional currency." One problem that the Confederates faced was counterfeiters. The Confederate money was easy to copy, so Northerners printed bills that looked like Confederate money and sent it to the South. Before long, Confederate money was everywhere and was not considered worth its value. There were so few $1 gold coins in the South by the end of the Civil War that they were worth $60 to $70 each. (The scarcer something is, the more expensive it is. A good example is top-quality diamonds and jewels, which are very expensive.)

By the end of the War, even strong supporters of the Confederacy knew their money wasn't worth anything, and there wasn't any chance of its value improving. Many Southerners began using Union money, when they could get it. Sometimes they had to get it through illegal means called a black market.

Look at the forms of money shown here. Circle the forms can you use today in the United States to pay for goods and services.

Civil War Facts

Ten hours after the first Civil War battle, 900 soldiers lay dead on the battlefield. Suddenly, there was a new awareness of exactly what war really was.

During the war, many arms and legs of soldiers were amputated (cut off) because doctors didn't know how to treat cannon wounds.

Many battles were fought on Virginia soil. In fact, more battles were fought in Virginia than in any other state—about 2,200 out of 4,000, or more than half!

General Lee surrendered Southern forces to Union General Ulysses S. Grant at Appomattox Court House. Instead of celebrating, most soldiers quietly returned home.

~ This book is not reproducible. ~

Section IX

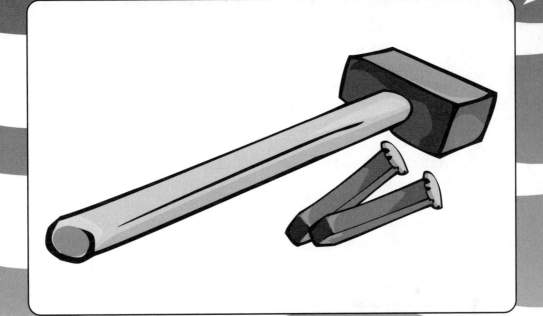

History and Civics: Effects of Reconstruction on American Life

Chapter 31

Standard USI.10a—Identify the provisions of the 13th, 14th, and 15th Amendments to the Constitution of the United States of America and their impact on the expansion of freedom in America. Correlates with USI.1a, USI.1b, USI.1c, USI.1d, and USI.1h.

Time for Some Additions

After the conclusion of the Civil War, which included freeing the slaves in the South, the Union's lawmakers realized that some changes were needed to the U.S. Constitution. Without changes, the ordeal of the war would have been for nothing. They added three amendments—the 13th, 14th, and 15th—to the U.S. Constitution.

- The 13th Amendment banned slavery in the United States and any of its territories.

- The 14th Amendment granted citizenship to all persons born in the United States and guarantees them equal protection under the law.

- The 15th Amendment ensures that the right to vote cannot be denied because of race, or color, or previous conditions of servitude.

These three amendments guarantee equal protection under the law for all citizens.

Section 1 of the 15th Amendment actually reads: "The right of citizens of the United States to vote shall not be denied or abridged by the United States or by any State on account of race, color, or previous condition of servitude."

Is this a primary source document?

____ YES ____ NO

Unscramble the words to help explain these amendments.

1. The 13th Amendment says, "Neither slavery nor involuntary servitude, except as a punishment for crime whereof the party shall have been duly convicted, shall exist within the United States, or any place subject to their jurisdiction."

    In other words, slavery was _____ (NEDBAN).

2. The 14th Amendment says, "All persons born or naturalized in the United States and subject to the jurisdiction thereof, are citizens of the United States and of the State wherein they reside."

    In other words, people born in the United States are _____ (ZICTINES) of the United States.

3. The 15th Amendment says, "The right of citizens of the United States to vote shall not be denied or abridged by the color, or previous condition of servitude."

    In other words, people could not be kept from voting just because they had been _____ (VASLES).

Who were the 13th, 14th, and 15th Amendments written for?

_____

_____

_____

_____

Here are some actual and proposed amendments. Determine if they are from the past or present. Write PAST or PRESENT under each, based on when it would have been important.

1. People 16 years old or younger are not allowed to drive cars. _____

2. People born in the United States are allowed to vote. _____

3. Slavery is not allowed in the United States. _____

4. A person younger than 18 will not be allowed to buy tobacco products. _____

The 13th Amendment was ratified on December 6, 1865. The 14th Amendment was passed on July 9, 1868, and the 15th Amendment passed on February 3, 1870.

Look at the brief description of the amendments below and put them in the order in which they were ratified.

1. _____ Former slaves shall be allowed to vote.

2. _____ Slavery is banned in the United States.

3. _____ Anyone born in the United States is considered a U.S. citizen.

Imagine you were a young African-American man in the year 1869. Write how you feel about:

1. slavery being banned: _____

2. becoming a citizen of the United States: _____

3. having the right to vote: _____

Chapter 32

Standard USI.10b—Describe the impact of Reconstruction policies on the South. Correlates with USI.1c and USI.1d.

Putting Things Back Together

After the Civil War, the nation went through a period called Reconstruction. It was a time when the broken nation was being put back together. Imagine trying to put back together a plate that was broken into 12 pieces: the Union and four border states were reunited with the 11 Southern states that had seceded.

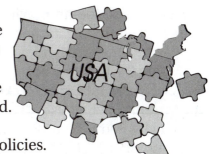

Many Southerners resented the Reconstruction policies. They were harsh and created problems in the South. For example:

- Southern military leaders could not hold political office.
- African Americans could hold political offices.
- Northern soldiers supervised the South.

Make a √ beside the time period(s) when a Southern military leader could have held a political office.

____ Before the Civil War   ____ During the Civil War   ____ After the Civil War

Profiting from Tragedy

During the Reconstruction period, thousands of white Northerners moved to the South. The South lay in destruction, and the newcomers saw a chance to make a lot of money by building new industries in the ruins. They opened mines, built factories, and replanted crops such as tobacco and cotton. The Southerners often called these people who were taking advantage of them "Yankee invaders." They were more commonly called "carpetbaggers" after the luggage made of carpets that they brought with them to the South.

Southern whites who worked with carpetbaggers were called "scalawags."

  ## Free at Last?

Another goal of Reconstruction was the attempt to give meaning to the freedom that the former slaves had achieved. African Americans gained equal rights as a result of the Civil Rights Act of 1866. Federal troops were authorized to enforce it.

While the Constitution guaranteed African Americans the right to vote, new laws were put into effect to keep them from voting in the South. One was called the "grandfather clause." Grandfather clauses required voters to have ancestors who had voted before 1867, which left out former slaves. Laws were also made that said people couldn't vote if they couldn't read or write, which also included most former slaves.

 Look at the statements below and decide who you think may have said them. Write the letter which applies before each statement.

A. Southern white   B. Carpetbagger   C. Former slave   D. Union soldier

1. ___ An election is coming up. I really want to vote, but I can't because I can't read or write.

2. ___ Losing the war was bad enough. My farm was destroyed and I have nothing, and now I have to put up with Yankee soldiers telling me what to do!

3. ___ After spending four years fighting, I thought I was through with wearing a uniform. Now, I am still stuck here in the South enforcing laws I didn't make with people who still think I'm the enemy.

4. ___ The South is a wreck. I think I can come down here and start a business and make some easy money.

Section X

Extra Credit

Fifty Nifty States

Can you match them all? Write each state's two letter abbreviation in the correct place on the map. See how many you can get right and add 'em up!

Alabama–AL
Alaska–AK
Arizona–AZ
Arkansas–AR
California–CA
Colorado–CO
Connecticut–CT
Delaware–DE
Florida–FL
Georgia–GA
Hawaii–HI
Idaho–ID
Illinois–IL

Indiana–IN
Iowa–IA
Kansas–KS
Kentucky–KY
Louisiana–LA
Maine–ME
Maryland–MD
Massachusetts–MA
Michigan–MI
Minnesota–MN
Mississippi–MS
Missouri–MO
Montana–MT

Nebraska–NE
Nevada–NV
New Hampshire–NH
New Jersey–NJ
New Mexico–NM
New York–NY
North Carolina–NC
North Dakota–ND
Ohio–OH
Oklahoma–OK
Oregon–OR
Pennsylvania–PA

Rhode Island–RI
South Carolina–SC
South Dakota–SD
Tennessee–TN
Texas–TX
Utah–UT
Vermont–VT
Virginia–VA
Washington–WA
West Virginia–WV
Wisconsin–WI
Wyoming–WY

~ This book is not reproducible. ~

United States History to 1877 Practice Test

1. What are continents?
   - A Small areas of land
   - B Large land masses surrounded by water
   - C Areas of land between two oceans
   - D Small island

2. What is the oldest mountain range in North America?
   - F Appalachian Mountains
   - G Blue Ridge Mountains
   - H Rocky Mountains
   - J Mount McKinley

3. What are the two oceans associated with the United States?
   - A Mediterranean and Arctic
   - B Arctic and Atlantic
   - C Atlantic and Pacific
   - D Atlantic and Indian

4. What determined how American Indians obtained their basic needs?
   - F Education
   - G Money
   - H Inheritance
   - J Environment

5. What nationalities were known for their exploration of North America?
   - A Libyan, Egyptian, and Sudanese
   - B English, French, and Spanish
   - C Chinese, Japanese, and Korean
   - D Swiss, Dutch, and German

6. What nationality of explorers sailed to West Africa on trade expeditions?
   - F Spanish
   - G English
   - H Japanese
   - J Portuguese

7. What were the main reasons that Europeans colonized America?
   - A Social and educational
   - B Urban and rural
   - C Political and agricultural
   - D Economic and religious

8. The three main regions of the colonies were—
   - F Northern, Southern, and Western.
   - G New England, Southern, and Western.
   - H New England, Mid-Atlantic, and Southern.
   - J Coastal, Mountain, and Lakeside.

9. Britain planned to pay for the French and Indian War by—
   - A taxing the colonies.
   - B stealing money from the French.
   - C selling land back to the Indians.
   - D fining the French.

10. The key philosophies of the Declaration of Independence are—
    - F life, liberty, and the pursuit of happiness.
    - G freedom of speech, religion, and the right to vote.
    - H right to vote and right to assemble.
    - J land, food, and clothing.

11. Who was the major author of the Declaration of Independence?
    - A Benjamin Franklin
    - B John Adams
    - C Thomas Jefferson
    - D John Locke

12. What battle was the turning point of the American Revolution?
    - F Concord and Lexington
    - G Cowpens
    - H Saratoga
    - J Manassas (Bull Run)

13. The first ten Amendments of the U.S. Constitution are called the—
    - A Bill of Rights.
    - B Constitution.
    - C Declaration of Independence.
    - D Monroe Doctrine.

14. What was the name of the great land buy made by Thomas Jefferson?
    - F The Louisiana Purchase
    - G The Nevada Territory
    - H The Big Land Buy
    - J The New Deal

15. People who spoke out against slavery were called—
    - A abolitionists.
    - B suffragists.
    - C antagonists.
    - D protagonists.

16. Which area of the United States relied most on agriculture?
    - F The Mid-Atlantic
    - G The North
    - H The South
    - J The West

17. The Emancipation Proclamation was supposed to—
    - A free prisoners of war.
    - B end the Civil War.
    - C establish stronger states' rights.
    - D free slaves who were living in Southern states.

18. What was the turning point of the Civil War?
    - F Firing on Fort Sumter
    - G The Battle of Gettysburg
    - H Surrender at Appomattox
    - J Lexington and Concord

19. What was the purpose of the 13th, 14th, and 15th Amendments to the U.S. Constitution?
    - A To address the issues of slavery
    - B To guarantee equal protection under the law for all citizens
    - C To give women the right to vote
    - D Both A and B

20. What was the period when the nation was reuniting after the Civil War called?
    - F Rebuilding
    - G Reunion
    - H Carpetbagger Era
    - J Reconstruction

Great job! You did it!

Section XI

Appendix

VIRGINIA

1492 — Christopher Columbus reaches the Americas

1513 — Vasco Núñez de Balboa sees the Pacific Ocean

1607 — 104 colonists establish a settlement at Jamestown

1608 — Samuel de Champlain founds Quebec

1620 — Pilgrims arrive at Plymouth

1732 — James Oglethorpe founds the colony of Georgia

1754 — French and Indian War begins

1763 — Proclamation of 1763

1765 — British pass Stamp Act

1768 — British soldiers are sent to Boston to keep order

1770 — The Boston Massacre

1773 — Boston Tea Party

1774 — First Continental Congress meets

1775 — Battles at Lexington and Concord

1776 — Colonists declare independence

1777 — Congress passes the Articles of Confederation

1781 — British surrender at Yorktown

1783 — Treaty of Paris recognizes the United States

1787 — Constitutional Convention assembles

1788 — U.S. Constitution is ratified; Bill of Rights is proposed

TIMELINE

1789 George Washington is elected first president

1791 Bill of Rights is ratified

1796 John Adams is elected president

1801 Thomas Jefferson is elected president

1803 Jefferson makes Louisiana Purchase from France

1812 United States declares war on England

1820 Congress passes Missouri Compromise

1823 Monroe writes Monroe Doctrine

1836 Texas becomes an independent republic

1846 United States declares war on Mexico

1848 United States gains Mexican lands in treaty with Mexico

1850 Compromise of 1850

1854 Kansas-Nebraska Acts

1860 Abraham Lincoln elected president; South Carolina secedes from the Union

1861 Civil War begins

1863 Abraham Lincoln signs Emancipation Proclamation

1865 Civil War ends; Lincoln is assassinated; 13th Amendment to the U.S. Constitution is ratified

1866 14th Amendment is ratified; Civil Rights Act of 1866 passes

1869 15th Amendment is ratified

USA Glossary

Abolitionist: someone who, before the Civil War, fought to end slavery

Artisan: a person skilled in an art form; a craftsperson

Compromise: settlement of an argument by each side giving up something

Continent: a large land mass surrounded by water

Guarantee: a promise

Indentured servant: person who could not afford to pay his way to America and would contract with a wealthy person to pay for the trip and then would pay the wealthy person back by working for him for a specified amount of time

Latitude: an imaginary line that joins points on the Earth's surface that are all equal distance north or south of the equator

Longitude: the angular distance east or west of the prime meridian

Proprietor: person who owns or operates a store or business

Ratify: to give formal approval to something so that it can become valid

Secede: to stop being a member of a group

Segregated: set apart from others; isolated

Sovereignty: the condition of having independent political power

Suffrage: the right to vote in political elections

Tariff: a list of taxes on goods that are brought into the country to be sold; goods made to be sold outside the country can also be tariffed

A Map of North America

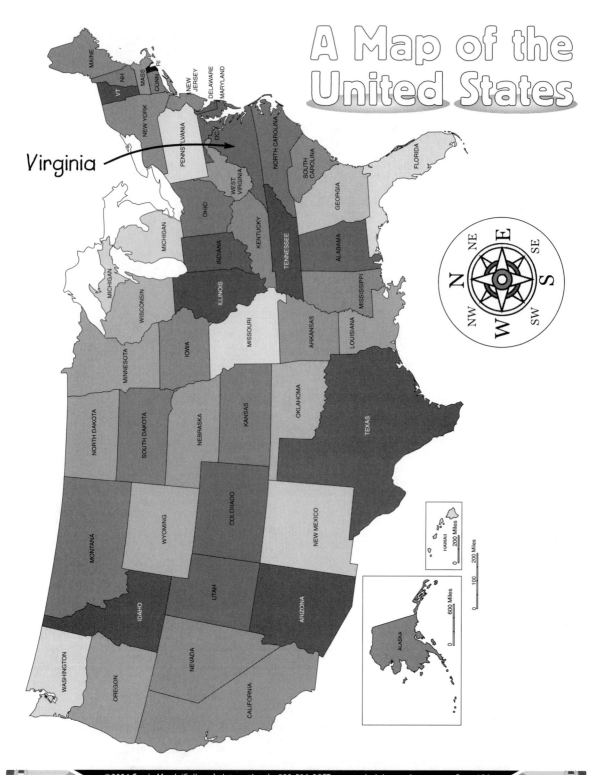

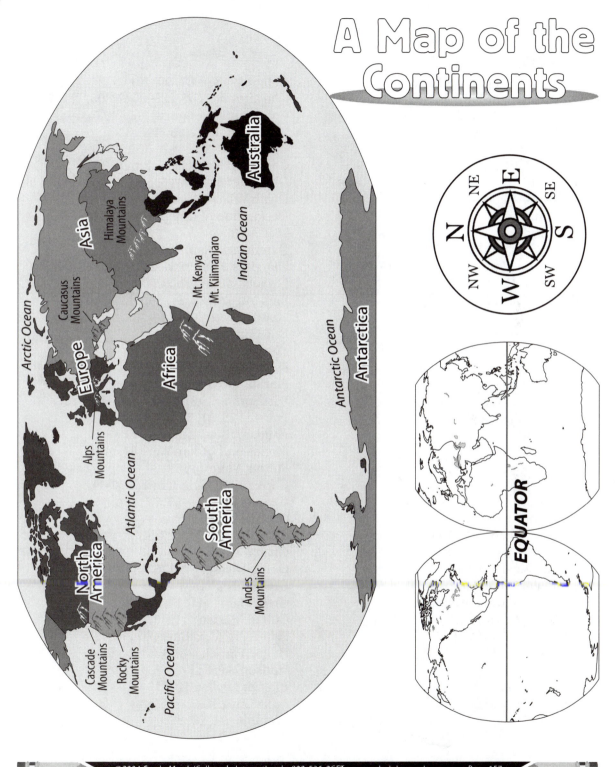

USA Index

13th Amendment 142–143
14th Amendment 142–143
15th Amendment 142–143
Adams, John 67, 90, 94, 96
Africa 8, 38-43, 53
African Americans 136, 144, 146
Alaska 21
American Indians 61
Anderson, Jo 108
Antarctica 8
Anthony, Susan B. 111–112
Appalachian Mountains 11, 12, 49
Appomattox Court House 127
Articles of Confederation 84–88
Asia 8, 21
Atlanta, Georgia 137
Atlantic Ocean 11,12, 13, 14, 40, 70, 104
Australia 8
Banneker, Benjamin 95
Barton, Clara 137
Basin and Range region 11
Bill of Rights 90, 95
Border states 122
Boston Massacre 71, 77–78
Boston Tea Party 73, 77–78
Burgesses, House of 67–68, 75–76
Cabot, John 28, 29, 31
California 11, 98, 104–105
Canada 11, 21, 28, 31, 103
Canadian Shield 11, 12
Champlain, Samuel de 19, 28, 29 30, 31
Charleston, South Carolina 130
Civil Rights Act of 1866 146
Coastal Plain 11, 12
Coastal Range 11, 12
Colorado River 13, 17
Columbia River 13, 17, 102
Compromise of 1850 120
Concord 77

Congress 86—87, 90, 101
Constitution, U.S. 89–90, 92–95, 114, 117
Continental Congress 67, 71, 75, 77
Continental Divide 11, 13
Cornwallis, Lord 67, 78
Coronado, Francisco 28, 29, 31
Davis, Jefferson 126
Death Valley 11, 13
Declaration of Independence 64–67, 71, 75, 77–78
Democratic Republicans 92–93
Douglass, Frederick 110–112, 126
Emancipation Proclamation 124–127, 130
England 28, 29, 31, 34, 57-58, 60, 62–81, 90, 102
Erie Canal 105
Europe 8
Federalists 92–93
Florida 98, 100
Fort Sumter, South Carolina 121, 127
France 28, 31, 34, 78, 80–81
Franklin, Benjamin 67, 71
French and Indian War 61
Fulton, Robert 109
Garrison, William Lloyd 110–112
George, King III 67, 77
Georgia 47, 108
Gettysburg 124, 127, 132
Ghana 38–44
Grant, Ulysses S. 126, 134
Great Lakes 13, 17
Great Plains 11, 12, 21, 23
Gulf of Mexico 11, 13, 14, 15
Hamilton, Alexander 92–94
Henry, Patrick 6–68
Hudson Bay 11
Interior Lowlands 11
Inuit 21, 23, 25
Iroquois 21, 23. 25

Jackson, Thomas "Stonewall" 136
Jamestown 46–47
Jefferson, Thomas 64-67, 75, 92–96, 98
Kansas-Nebraska Act 120
Kentucky 61
Kwakiutl 21, 23. 25
La Salle, Robert 31
Lee, Robert E. 124–127, 140
Lewis and Clark 17, 19, 94, 98–100
Lexington 77–78
Lincoln, Abraham 118, 120–127
Locke, John 62–64, 74
Louisiana Purchase 95
Madison, James 89–90, 92, 94-96
Mali 38-44
Manassas 127
Manifest Destiny 105
Maryland 85
Massachusetts Bay Colony 46–47
Mayflower Compact 46-47
McCormick, Cyrus 108–109
Mexico 17, 104
Mid-Atlantic 49, 51, 53
Mississippi River 13, 17, 98, 131
Missouri Compromise 119
Missouri River 13, 17, 98
Monroe Doctrine 94-96
Monroe, James 94–96
New England 49, 51, 53
New Orleans, Louisiana 130
New York 85
North 114—146
North America 8, 11
Oglethorpe, James 47–48
Ohio River 13, 17
Oregon 102, 105–106
Pacific Ocean 11, 12, 13, 14, 19, 98–100, 103
Paine, Thomas 67, 74
Parliament 61
Pennsylvania 46–47, 85, 132
Pilgrims 46, 48

Plymouth 46
Portugal 28, 31, 33
Proclamation of 1763 61
Pueblo 21, 23, 25
Puritans 46
Quakers 46
Quebec 28, 31
Reconstruction 145–146
Revere, Paul 73, 77
Richmond, Virginia 128, 137
Rio Grande 13, 101, 104
Roanoke Island 46
Rocky Mountains 11, 12, 98–100, 105
Sacagawea 100
Saratoga 78
Savannah, Georgia 47, 130
Sherman, William T. 130, 137
Sioux 21, 23, 25
Smalls, Robert 138
Snake River 99
Songhai 38–44
South 49, 51, 53, 114–146
South America 8
Spain 28, 31, 34, 78, 80–81
Stamp Act 61, 71
Stanton, Elizabeth Cady 111–112
Tennessee 61
Texas 17, 98. 101–102
Treaty of Paris 78
Truth, Isabel Sojourner 110–112
Tubman, Harriet 109–112
Vicksburg, Mississippi 127, 131, 136
Virginia 47, 75–76, 85, 124, 127–129, 140
Virginia Company 46
Virginia Plan 89
Washington, D.C. 95, 128, 134
Washington, George 67, 76. 92, 94, 96
West Africa 31, 33, 38–44
Wheatley, Phillis 69–70
Whitney, Eli 108–109
Yorktown 78

About the Author...

Carole Marsh has been writing about Virginia and the United States for more than 20 years. She is the author of the popular Virginia State Stuff series for young readers and creator, along with her son, Michael Longmeyer, of Virginia Facts and Factivities, a CD-ROM widely used in Virginia schools. The author of more than 100 Virginia books and other supplementary educational materials for young people, including My First Pocket Guide: Virginia. Marsh correlates her Virginia materials to Virginia's Standards of Learning. Many of her books and other materials have been inspired by or requested by Virginia teachers and librarians.

Note to Teachers
The Answer Key for this workbook is included in *The Virginia Experience United States I Teacher Resource Book*. If you did not purchase the Teacher Resource Book and need the Answer Key, please call 800-536-2438 and we will fax or mail one to you.